Drama 7–11

Although drama is becoming increasingly important as an effective learning medium within the primary school, there is currently much confusion and anxiety about what exactly it is, and how it should be taught.

This book is a practical guide to teaching drama and provides a clear and coherent framework together with a theoretical underpinning which will allow teachers to create their own lessons from an informed standpoint and maximize the learning potential.

Drama is variously seen as a way of teaching other subjects, an art form in its own right, a series of games and exercises, both large and small performances, a therapeutic tool and an elaborated form of play.

The authors propose a curriculum for drama that combines the diverse references in the various documents of the National Curriculum whilst at the same time identifying the unique qualities specific to the subject which can form a coherent framework for teachers to adopt.

Central to the book are a range of techniques, examples and activities that will provide a firm foundation for the teaching of drama, give confidence to those who have little or no experience and allow development for others who may have already acquired some.

Neil Kitson is based at the School of Education at Leicester University and **Ian Spiby** is Leader of the Performance Studies Division at Nene College, Northampton.

Curriculum in primary practice series
General editor: Clive Carré

The Curriculum in primary practice series is aimed at students and qualified teachers looking to improve their practice within the context of the National Curriculum. The large format, easy to use texts are interactive, encouraging teachers to engage in professional development as they read. Each contains:

- Summaries of essential research
- Transcripts of classroom interactions for analysis and discussion
- Activities for individual and group use

While all primary teachers will find these books useful, they are designed with the needs of teachers of the 7 to 11 age group particularly in mind.

Other titles include:

Science 7–11
Clive Carre and Carrie Ovens

History 7–11
Jon Nichol with Jacqui Dean

Music 7–11
Sarah Hennessy

English 7–11
David Wray

Religious Education 7–11
Terence Copley

Art 7–11
Linda Green and Robin Mitchell

Drama 7–11

Developing primary teaching skills

Neil Kitson and Ian Spiby

London and New York

First published 1997
by Routledge
11 New Fetter Lane, London EC4P 4EE

Simultaneously published in the USA and Canada
by Routledge
29 West 35th Street, New York, NY 10001

Typeset in Palatino by Solidus (Bristol) Limited
Printed and bound in Great Britain by
Butler & Tanner Ltd, Frome and London

British Library Cataloguing in Publication Data
A catalogue record for this book is available from the British Library

Library of Congress Cataloging in Publication Data
A catalogue record for this book has been requested

ISBN 0–415–14184–2

Contents

Illustrations

Introduction

Three teachers of Year 5 children in three schools in different parts of the country are teaching a drama lesson on the theme of 'Bullying'. Chris Johnson in Birmingham is newly qualified. She is interested in drama and did some at college. Derek Howes in Kent has been teaching for twenty-eight years. He doesn't find drama a congenial subject to teach. As he says, he's not a very 'dramatic' person, but he does feel it's important for his children to have some experience of it – and they enjoy it. Terri Routhwaite in Newcastle has been teaching for thirteen years and is a drama specialist. She studied drama at college, is a keen member of an amateur theatrical society and has attended a number of INSET courses. We're going to follow Chris's lesson in detail and look at the way Derek and Terri use alternative strategies.

Chris Johnson teaches her drama lesson in the classroom, not in the Hall. She finds it a more intimate space with less likelihood of interruptions and early on in her career she discovered how, with a little training, the children could quickly move the tables and chairs to one side to leave a good space in the middle. She begins her lesson like all her drama lessons, sitting on the floor with the children in a circle and as always she asks them to remind her what the 'rules' of drama are. The children offer ideas: in drama no one is ever wrong; in drama we always listen to one another; in drama Miss Johnson will always try to make it as interesting and exciting as she can; in drama everyone agrees not to be silly or disruptive; and so on. The children and teacher agree that they will follow these rules – and so the drama starts.

Derek and Terri operate in much the same way but with slight differences. Derek uses his classroom for drama but Terri has a spare classroom which has been converted into a drama studio. It has black-out facilities and a couple of portable stage lights. She starts sitting with the children in a circle on the floor but does not feel the need to go through the 'rules' of drama. They are quite used to what is expected of them and the whole atmosphere of the special drama space reinforces this. Derek refuses to sit on the floor with the kids, saying that if he got down there, his rheumatism would probably prevent him from ever getting up again. Instead he sits on a low chair purloined from the infant department. He too no longer feels the need to remind his class what is expected of them in drama.

Chris reads out a poem, 'Four o'clock Friday'* by John Foster.

Four o'clock, Friday, I'm home at last
Time to forget the week that has passed

On Monday, at break, they stole my ball
And threw it over the playground wall.

On Tuesday morning, I came in late,
But they were waiting behind the gate.

On Wednesday afternoon, in games
They threw mud at me and called me names.

Yesterday, they laughed after the test
'Cause my marks were lower than the rest.

Today, they trampled my books on the floor
And I was kept in because I swore.

Four o'clock, Friday, at last I'm free,
For two whole days they can't get at me.

Chris invites responses to the poem from the class and then begins to question the children. Who is the supposed writer of the poem? Is it a boy or girl? Why do they think that? What sort of person is it? What's happening to him or her? How does he or she feel about it? Do they think he or she tells anyone what's happening? Is he or she doing anything about it? If not, why not? Would the class decide who the person is and give him or her a name. They decide it's a boy called Jason. (Chris doesn't spend long on this choosing and naming activity. While she was at college she videoed one of her drama lessons and, watching the playback, discovered she'd spent nearly fifteen minutes with the class deciding, by democratic vote, if a farmer character they were creating should be named Mr Smith or Mr Smithson. She still cringes with embarrassment at the remembrance of it!)

Derek starts his lesson by reading out an entry from a diary, written supposedly by a child who is being bullied and covering much the same material as the poem.

Terri, on the other hand begins by taking the role of a worried parent on the telephone, talking to someone at the school while the children overhear the conversation. Rather cleverly she doesn't make it obvious that she thinks her child is being bullied, but rather hints at it, planting clues which the children will subsequently have to work at to sort out.

Chris then sets a chair in the middle of the circle, borrows someone's coat and places it on the chair. She says that, for the moment, the coat on the chair will represent Jason and that everyone else in the class is going to be someone who knows him: family, schoolfriends, teachers, neighbours. It doesn't matter if for the purposes of the exercise he has three mothers or two fathers – what is important is that they all have something to say about Jason. The technique is known as statementing. She invites them to stand in relation to the chair according to how well they know him. So, for example, his mother(s) might stand in front and close, while the man who owns the newsagent shop where he buys sweets might be behind and at a distance. Chris then goes round the room and as she touches each child on the shoulder, they make a statement about Jason. She reminds them beforehand to listen very carefully to what everyone else says because they are together building up a picture of him. Afterwards they sit back in the circle and feed back to the teacher what they now know. It is at this point that Chris can sort out any problems with diametrically opposing facts by asking them to decide which they want to be 'true' for this drama. She makes sure that people whose ideas are about to be jettisoned are acknowledged and their permission asked.

Derek adopts a different device known as 'role-on-the-wall'. He draws the outline of a figure on the board and invites the children to give words or phrases which describe the bullied boy. A composite picture is therefore made up.

Terri is more sophisticated. She divides the class into small groups and asks them to devise questions that they would like answered by the Jason character. After a while she then takes the role of Jason and the class questions 'him' – a technique often described as hot-seating. Terri is able to build tension by giving certain information, sidestepping questions, hinting at other facts. In other words, as with the telephone conversation, she makes the children work at finding out. The more they have to work, the more intrigued and involved they become.

Having established some information about the bullied boy, Chris now wants to make the incidents of bullying more real to the children so she asks them in small groups to devise a short (thirty-second) scene that depicts a bullying memory of Jason's. While they prepare the scene, they enact the role of the bullies without an actual Jason to practise on (!) because when they each show their scene, Miss Johnson will come into it in role as Jason while all the other children will play the role of bystanders, on-lookers or witnesses to the incident. Chris learned on teaching practice that simply asking the children to present their completed scenes group by group often meant that no one watched except her! The children need a *purpose* in order to get them to watch.

Derek asks the children to do a series of still images or tableaux of a bullying incident and as each group presents theirs, the rest of the class gathers round and attempts to interpret what is going on.

Terri also asks the children to work in small groups, but they perform a scene from one of Jason's nightmares. Because they have had a lot of experience they are able to manipulate the dramatic form and get away from everyday realism. The scenes consist of frightening images, repeated words and phrases, strange shapes and so on. When the time comes to show the results of their work, Terri places the children round the edge of the classroom and she moves from group to group, in role as the frightened Jason. Only when she approaches a group does it come to life and thus the total scene is unified while she controls the dramatic pace and tension, moving now slowly, now quickly from group to group.

Having established something about the person being bullied, Chris feels that it is time to introduce the bully. She is keen not to encourage the children to think in stereotypes and decides therefore that the best way to do this is through narration – in other words she tells a story in the present tense, while the children sitting in the circle listen. It goes something like this:

Andrew lives at home with his Mum and Dad and two older brothers. It's quite comfortable at home – he's got lots of toys and games to play with, he's got his own room with a television and there's always plenty to eat. But his Mum and Dad are very strict – especially his Dad. His Dad is a big man – and his brothers are big as well – while Andrew is quite small for his age. His Dad has brought up his brothers, Michael and David, to be very tough – and they are. They never ever cry, even if they're hurt or really upset about something and Andrew's learned that he must never cry as well. Once when he was younger he fell out of a tree and hurt himself quite badly. But his brothers just laughed and his father said he was ashamed of him making such a fuss. He should try to act like a real boy and not be like a soft girl! He threatened to make him wear a dress to school if he couldn't behave like a boy. Because he's younger and smaller than his brothers he can't do things as well as they can, and they're always making fun of him – jeering and laughing. Andrew doesn't think very much of himself – he doesn't think he's very clever or good at anything. But at school, he boasts to the other children – especially about his brothers, how tough they are. And he bullies children who are weaker than he is.

Derek opts for a narration as well.

Terri takes the role of Andrew, performing a monologue. She starts by telling the children that she wants them to meet another character in the drama and she says that what she's going to do is speak this character's thoughts out loud. She doubts if he would ever *say* these things to anyone. As she sits in a chair in front of them, the role begins. The information given in the monologue is much the same as that contained in the narration but the effect is immeasurably more powerful. She sits in a chair, head down, twisting her fingers, voice barely above a whisper. You could hear a pin drop!

After her narration, Chris invites the class to talk about Andrew and discuss the problem of bullying. She suggests that they take a group role as the headteacher of Jason and Andrew's school to interview him. (A group role is where a number of people share the responsibility for one character. In this case the whole class will *all* be the headteacher.) They set up the classroom with chairs in a large semicircle and with one chair in front for Andrew. Chris takes the role of Andrew and in the quite lengthy interview that follows she adopts a very defensive stance, denying everything, putting the blame on others and so on. After a while, when the children are clearly getting nowhere and before their frustration leads to boredom, she suggests that another way might be to have a 'dream-sequence tribunal' where Andrew *has* to tell the truth. They set up the tribunal in terms of the layout of furniture, and Chris asks them to decide on individual roles for themselves, either as children who have been bullied (including Jason) or as teachers, Mums and Dads, social workers, etc. She asks for a volunteer to be the Chair of the tribunal and one of the more confident girls agrees. They discuss how things are going to be conducted and then they begin. Chris takes the role of Andrew, telling the truth. She feels that it is important that she takes this role because she doesn't want a simple solution to the problem – it is too easy for Andrew and Jason to end up shaking hands and Andrew promising to be good in future. So although Andrew tells the truth, he nevertheless cannot promise that he will not bully again. Chris, in role as Andrew, makes the character as psychologically complex as she judges the children can take.

Out of role the class sits down to discuss the drama and reflect on it, particularly with regard to the question: 'How do we stop bullying?'

Derek decides to set up a staff meeting with the teachers of Jason and Andrew's school. Taking the role of the headteacher, Derek explains to the staff that Jason ran away from school and by chance, he (the headteacher) spotted him, picked him up in his car and took him home. The 'teachers' are asked their advice. Has anyone observed anything which might account for Jason's unhappiness? What is the solution to the problem? They decide that they should interview Jason with his parents and then Andrew with his parents. Volunteers from the class agree to take on these roles while everyone else takes the part of the interviewing teachers. Derek, in role still as the headteacher, is the Chair of the meeting. At the end of the drama some kind of reconciliation between Jason and Andrew is effected.

Terri opts for a convention known as forum theatre. Two volunteers agree to take the roles of Jason and Andrew and supported by the rest of the class (and Terri) they begin to enact a bullying scene very slowly. At each point in the interaction, the class offers advice to the players about what to say, how to stand, etc. It is quite permissible for another member of the class to take the role of Andrew or Jason for some or all of the time. Because of Terri's skill as a drama teacher, she gradually brings into the scene other members of the class in role as members of Andrew's gang, sympathizers of Jason, and more importantly, children who are witnessing the bullying incident but who do nothing. Gradually she turns the spotlight away from the bully and bullied to them. Why are they doing nothing? What *could* they do? By the end of the forum theatre, the children in the class are facing the rather unpalatable fact that they *all* bear responsibility for the prevention of bullying. When they sit down to reflect upon 'what happened in the drama' their thinking and their perceptions have been moved.

These three versions of the Bullying drama are fairly typical of the kind of lessons currently taught by teachers with an up-to-date understanding of drama-in-education. They cover a range of the techniques used (such as 'still images', 'hot-seating', 'conscience alley' and 'forum theatre' – for descriptions of such conventions see Figure 4.1, p. 62) and they also indicate a range of skills on the part of the teachers. While all three teachers teach good lessons, Derek Howes adopts the simplest approach with the greatest amount of 'safety'. Chris Johnson's lesson is still fairly safe but contains a certain amount of risk and indicates a higher level of skill and understanding while Terri Routhwaite shows a sophistication and awareness of both dramatic techniques and sound educational practice which puts her among the top rank of drama teachers.

It is our intention in this book to show you how to teach drama lessons somewhere at least around the level of Derek Howes and Chris Johnson but at the same time keeping a weather eye on Terri Routhwaite in order to be able to progress and improve as you gain in confidence and experience. We've adopted these 'Derek' and 'Chris' models because they are the sort of people to whom this book is primarily addressed. Derek is competent, experienced and enthusiastic but like hundreds of similar teachers he admits to some confusion and lack of confidence when he faces a class for a drama lesson. There are a number of reasons for this. Firstly the one mentioned earlier about his feeling that he doesn't have a natural aptitude – he's not a 'dramatic' person. We feel this is a misapprehension and we'll be dealing with it shortly. Secondly, since Derek trained in the early 1960s and perhaps just as importantly since he went to school in the 1940s and 1950s there have been huge changes in thinking about drama in schools. We'll be dealing with that also. Chris, on the other hand, is in her first year of teaching. She's had some drama-in-education experience at her teacher-training establishment but as a non-specialist, not nearly enough. She had one two-hour session in her first year and three two-hour sessions in Year 3 – and that she understands is typical of provision in most teacher-education institutes. She therefore feels under-trained in this area, lacking confidence and not absolutely clear how she can maximize drama's potential with her class. She is reasonably comfortable teaching drama lessons that other people have written for her but doesn't know how to plan them for herself, based on a subject or theme of her own choice. Instinctively, she has the feeling that her class has certain needs that drama could cater for but she doesn't know how to use it to meet those needs. This will be one of the main thrusts of the book. Our method is to take you step by step through the basic techniques of drama teaching, providing exercises and examples to try out in your own class. We want to de-mystify the subject and show that it can be taught by any primary teacher, not just those with special arcane knowledge and skills.

Drama in schools is riddled with misunderstandings – and we will go into some of them in more detail in the next Unit. At this point it is simply sufficient to say that the subject is often regarded as an extra to the normal curriculum – a frill that can be dispensed with if other things are too pressing. We want to show in this book that drama is an essential part of the curriculum and an extremely powerful tool for learning.

 ACTIVITY 0.1

Look at the Programme of Study for National Curriculum Key Stage 2 English, Speaking and Listening. You'll find a copy of it in Appendix I at the end of this book.

Now go back and read through the three versions of the drama lesson on Bullying at the beginning of this Unit. Place a tick against each of the items in the Programme of Study that you think the pupils in those lessons would have engaged with.

Even from this preliminary exercise it will be clear that something more than just 'playing around' was occurring in the drama – and we mention the phrase 'playing around' because it is a common stick used to beat advocates of drama. ('Oh, in drama they just play around.')We will see later that there is certainly an element of play in drama but it is used by the teacher for active learning purposes.

Another, more subtle, criticism is: 'But in drama, aren't you just teaching them to act' – the implication being that it's a waste of time unless they are going to be actors when they grow up. The answer is that in drama we are not teaching children how to 'act' but to understand the art form of drama and by extension, theatre – a very different thing. Again more of this later. Before we do leave it, however, it is worth mentioning a widespread fear that large numbers of non-specialist teachers hold. Many echo Derek Howes' fears – they are not good at acting and therefore can't teach drama. They are particularly afraid of taking a role themselves. We want to show that in order to teach drama successfully, you don't have to be an actor. Role-playing is something we do every day of our lives. I tell someone at work about something amusing that my young daughter said, after stamping her foot: 'I'll wun away I will. (Pause) *Can* I wun away?' When I tell them, I take on the role of my daughter – I give a rough imitation of the way she spoke; I may even mimic some of her gestures or her stance as she spoke. But my listener doesn't think for an instant that I'm *acting* my daughter, 'getting inside the part' as it were. What I do for that moment is to take on an *attitude*. I remain myself quite clearly all the time. Think of the last time you pretended to get cross with your class. You weren't really angry – merely playing the role of 'cross teacher' . That method, in its basic form is all that is actually required in drama. Of course you can do a great deal more and the more skilled you become the more you will use an understanding of the way drama and theatre works.

ACTIVITY 0.2

Look back over the Bullying drama, particularly the parts where Terri Routhwaite's version of the lesson is described. Write down a list of the dramatic and theatrical things she does. Try to imagine yourself doing those things. Above all, try to think of doing them as *yourself* rather than 'acting a part'. You may find this difficult or even impossible but we hope that by the end of the book, if you return to this exercise, it won't seem nearly as daunting.

This book can be used as part of an INSET course or by an individual. The exercises have been designed so that either one person or a group can do them. In many ways a group is better because it allows for an exchange of ideas, but a lone reader can also get a great deal from the exercises. We want to encourage people to do some drama in their own classrooms and it is quite possible to build up confidence step by step if you have never tried any before. For such people we would recommend starting by doing something for five minutes rather than an hour-long epic. Begin with techniques that involve tight control of the class. You can move to a more open approach later. Above all we want you by the time you have worked through the book to have experienced the marvellous power of drama – the unique way it grabs kids and makes them face problems, often life and death problems, not only as if they are real but as if they really matter.

*'Four o'clock Friday' by John Foster © 1991 John Foster. First published in *A Fifth Poetry Book* compiled by John Foster, Oxford University Press, 1991.

Unit 1

Drama-in-education

In the Introduction we commented on how drama is often seen as a fringe subject in schools. Very often it shares this perception with the other arts: dance and music as well as the whole range of activities that come under the umbrella of fine art. Of course, with art and music which are named specifically in the National Curriculum, such marginalization has receded somewhat. But what makes drama different from its fellow artistic subjects is that there is considerable confusion about what it actually is. This has even extended into bitterly contested debates among drama theorists and true to the tradition of what everyone expects from 'dramatic' people, there have been accusations of defamation of character and threats of court action! Unlike in the cases of art and music though, the National Curriculum has not helped the matter, for where drama *is* mentioned, many practitioners find themselves at odds with the way it is described and the assumptions made about it. This, despite the fact that in Activity 0.1 in the Introduction, it is likely that you found the Bullying drama to have covered many of the aspects mentioned in the Speaking and Listening Programme. Little wonder then that newcomers, confronted by a bewildering array of types of drama and competing methodologies, are tempted to throw up their hands in despair and turn to another subject to teach.

In this Unit we are going to pick our way through this minefield so that by the end we will have an understanding of what drama in schools is about, why we should teach it and what we are aiming for when we do teach it. It's probably the most difficult Unit in the book but we think it is important because it will give a sound basis on which you can create your own drama lessons rather than simply rely on those that have been created and written up in books. To help us through the Unit, and so that you don't develop theory-indigestion, we shall be referring back from time to time to the Bullying lessons. First of all, however, try the following:

ACTIVITY 1.1

The nature of school drama

Brainstorm all the images which come to mind when the phrase 'school drama' is mentioned. If you are in a group, share the images and make a list of all the different activities that come under this heading.

You can now turn to the end of the Unit to see a detailed list of those we've thought of, although it is very likely that you have thought of activities not included there. In any case your list will probably be quite long and comprise a surprisingly wide variety of activities and pursuits, some of which appear at first sight to bear only a remote relationship to one another. Contrast the picture of small children playing in a pretend corner (called in pre-politically correct times a Wendy House) with older children engaged in a Board Room simulation; 'music and movement' with a school play; personal development games and exercises with drama club improvisations; a nativity play with a problem-solving role play; choral speaking with a puppet play.

 ACTIVITY 1.2

Drama experience (Part A)

Think about your own personal experiences of drama, both when you were at school, at college or university and during your teacher-training. Try to pinpoint the moments that were i) most enjoyable, ii) most meaningful and iii) most uncomfortable. Once again, if you are part of a group, share these experiences and see if you can isolate some common threads in the three types of experiences.

The uncomfortable experiences are probably the most vivid. A colleague of ours recalls at her teacher-training establishment being asked in a drama class to pick up an imaginary baby bird with a broken wing and hold it gently in her skirt. Then, with her fellow students, she had to go outside, acutely aware of the smirks of passers-by to place the bird carefully on the grass. One of the present writers as a student, attended a drama session conducted by Peter Slade (see p. 101) in which the whole group was made to run around the hall with arms held out pretending to be aeroplanes. Both of these activities seem to us to reveal fundamental misunderstandings about the nature of drama and we will be returning to them later. But they do go a little way towards an understanding of why teachers of drama have traditionally been seen as colourful, eccentric characters who ask their pupils to do outrageous, embarrassing things.

The enjoyable experiences on the other hand are likely to be concerned with the putting on of a play: the sense of camaraderie, of a special occasion, the excitement of appearing before an audience – that feeling of being involved in a special time somehow outside the boundaries of ordinary everyday life. While a great deal of learning takes place during this time, meaningful or learning experiences most often recalled are to do with drama sessions not directly connected with performance. They can be part of the rehearsal process or a drama lesson and are most frequently associated with an emotional experience. Something that happens within the drama touches us personally and even while the subject might be upsetting (the loss of a loved one for example), strangely it is at the same time enjoyable. Before going any further, it might be worthwhile considering the three types of experiences in connection with the Bullying dramas.

 ACTIVITY 1.3

Drama experience (Part B)

What were the moments during the drama(s) that you think the children found

a) most uncomfortable;
b) most enjoyable;
c) most meaningful.

How far do you think that a), b) and c) mix? Can you, for example, point to moments when all three experiences were occurring simultaneously?
    What was the *nature* of the discomfort, the enjoyment or the meaningfulness? How does this compare with what you remember of your own experiences?

These three types of experiences which in some ways are at odds with one another but in others (we hope you have discovered) seem to be intertwined, go some way towards accounting for the confusion over the precise nature of the subject.

    A further confusion is highlighted by the number of activities listed under the name of 'drama' in Activity 1.1 at the beginning of the Unit and one of the reasons for this is because the philosophy of drama-in-education has developed and changed in the years since 1945. In fact there was no coherent *written* philosophy at all until just over fifteen years ago. Drama is often regarded as a somewhat new subject on the school curriculum despite the fact that its use in education goes back at least as far as the sixteenth century. However, until after the Second World War, with a few exceptions, it was firmly linked to both elocution and the performance of written texts – especially Shakespeare; hence the term 'Speech and Drama', still seen, amazingly, as a heading in the appointments columns of the *Times Educational Supplement*.

KEY POINTS

Drama is in a confused state.

It means different things to different people.

Their experiences of drama are variously uncomfortable, enjoyable or meaningful – or a combination of all three!

THE DEVELOPMENT OF DRAMA THINKING

In the 1950s and early 1960s the ideas of the drama adviser Peter Slade became fashionable, spread by the publication in 1954 of his book *Child Drama*. He argued strongly that child drama was an art form in its own right and quite different from theatre and performance. The teacher's job was to encourage or allow to happen what is essentially a natural process. It is unfortunate that much of the book is written in a rather fey, poetic style which has obscured for later readers much of what he has to say that makes a lot of sense. Be that as it may, Slade must bear some responsibility for a phrase which has been used ever since as yet another stick to beat drama teachers – 'free expression'.

Slade's ideas were superseded by those of Brian Way who as a drama practitioner felt that the fundamental purpose of the subject was the personal development of the participants. Literally dozens of books were spawned as a result which gave hundreds of ideas for exercises and (later on) games to be played in the name of drama. One of these books *A 100+ Ideas for Drama* is still in print and can be found on many a staffroom bookshelf. Non-interference by the teacher, however, still continued to hold sway and gave rise to the notorious 'bum on the radiator' style of teaching whereby the teacher would divide the class into groups, give them a subject to make up a play about (for example a plane crash), sit at the side (perhaps doing a little marking the while) as they prepared it, then watch while one by one the groups presented their finished product. End of lesson.

KEY POINTS

The plot so far:

You let the kids do their own thing – express themselves freely. On the other hand you give them exercises or play games so they can develop personally.

It's nothing to do with performing but when they've made up plays in groups without teacher interference, expressing themselves freely, they perform them to one another.

THE NEW THEORETICIANS

In 1970, the BBC broadcast a highly influential film in their *Omnibus* series entitled *Three Looms Waiting* about Dorothy Heathcote, a lecturer in drama at Newcastle University, and indeed, if what she says in the film were to be studied carefully by every present-day, quarrelling theorist, the basis for such quarrels would largely disappear. We will be returning to these ideas later but what was taken from the film at the time was the fact that Mrs Heathcote would apparently go into a class, ask the children what they wanted 'to do a play about' and from their suggestions create a spell-binding drama with them – just like that! Even more alarmingly, she actually joined in the drama and took part herself. The result was that many drama teachers, including one of the present writers, simply gave up in despair. Drama was difficult enough when it was thoroughly planned without the strain of spinning marvellous things out of thin air. The common reaction to her work was, 'Yes, what she does is wonderful but I could never work like that', thus reinforcing the idea that drama teaching was only for a special kind of charismatic person and not for ordinary folk like you and me.

In 1979, another university lecturer, Gavin Bolton, this time at Durham, published a seminal book, *Towards a Theory of Drama in Education* and his ideas together with Heathcote's held sway for the next ten years. Basically Bolton's work was taken to advocate drama as a medium for learning. With the aid of the teacher adopting a role in the drama, children would be presented with situations in which it was necessary to solve problems ('How do we persuade the Squire to let us build a railway through his land?' for example). As such it was seen to be a very powerful and effective method for teaching other subjects, particularly those that concerned social, moral or historical issues. Despite the fact that if we look carefully at Bolton's writings we find a somewhat different story, such drama came to be seen as separate from theatre and in certain quarters 'performance' became a dirty word. In some schools and colleges, so extreme was the view that drama was a *method* rather than a subject, that its eradication from the timetable was advocated by the very people who were in favour of it. It was to be an all-purpose method. There was no part of the curriculum that could not be taught through drama.

Meanwhile a number of people began to develop the Bolton/Heathcote way of teaching to make it accessible to ordinary teachers. No longer did a teacher have to ask 'What do you want to do a play about?' but drama could now be planned as part of the ongoing classroom curriculum. The work of the practitioner Jonothan Neelands on developing a series of conventions ('still image', 'conscience alley', etc.) brought drama further within the reach of the non-specialist teacher.

KEY POINTS

The plot thickens:

Dorothy Heathcote joins in the drama with the kids and makes it up as she goes along. Gavin Bolton supplies the theory – drama is for learning. It catches on in a big way – performing is out.

> David Hornbrook attacks and says get back to performing and learning about theatre. Both sides claim 'drama is an art form'.
>
> Quarrels and tantrums on all sides.

Given that in our primary schools, teachers will have been variously trained from the 1950s to the present day, their drama experience is likely to have been influenced by any one of a number of conflicting ideas and fashions and, unless they have taken active steps to keep up with the latest developments, their drama teaching will probably appear to be frozen in time. This is particularly true when we remember that drama is accorded a low priority status by many teachers. In fact the phenomenon of being totally out of step with contemporary drama practice can be true of a whole school. We recently came across the drama policy of a primary school in the north of England. The school itself, far from being old fashioned, enjoys a high profile and in 1994 was the recipient of an 'Investors in People' award. The drama document, however, is firmly rooted in the ideas of Peter Slade and Brian Way and could thus be regarded as at least thirty years out of date.

On the other hand, it does not serve a useful purpose simply to dismiss out of hand the ideas of earlier practitioners, for while in any subject it is tempting to do this, their work frequently adds up cumulatively to the position we find ourselves in today. This is particularly true of drama and while we would not wish to advocate the wholesale adoption of the philosophy of any one person from the past, they undoubtedly all have something to say.

 ACTIVITY 1.4

Identifying attitudes and viewpoints

The following example is an imaginary conversation between a group of teachers, trained at different times. They are talking about what they feel drama-in-education is and quite clearly have different ideas. Read the conversation and try to match the thoughts of the teachers with the following three practitioners: Peter Slade, Gavin Bolton, David Hornbrook.

 Teacher One
I'm very suspicious of all this free expression stuff. I really think we should be teaching children about the great heritage of dramatic literature we have in this country

Teacher Two
But that can be so dry for young children. It has its place at secondary school but children should be given the opportunity to express themselves

in drama. They should be allowed to 'be'. We're there simply to provide the wherewithal so that they can put their ideas into creative form.

Teacher Three
Surely they could do that sort of drama in the playground by themselves? Time spent on the curriculum is so precious that we've really got to justify everything we do. And drama seems such a good way of teaching other subjects.

Teacher Two
Wouldn't you just be telling them what to do though? I believe the ideas should come from them. And they couldn't do *my* drama in the playground. I'm there to help and advise, although I certainly wouldn't see myself as interfering.

Teacher One
Your ideas seem to me to be getting away from the real idea of drama and just letting them play. All the drama they are ever likely to see has started from a script, then been rehearsed and performed. I firmly believe that's what we should be doing.

Teacher Three
You might be able to do that in a mechanical way, but I wonder how much the kids would get out of it? Unless they can have an imagined experience that means something to them then aren't we wasting our time?

When you've had a go at this activity, look at the end of the Unit where you'll see the 'answers'. However, what we've done is to simplify and stereotype the three attitudes to drama-in-education. Look now at Appendix II where you will see extracts from the writings of Peter Slade, Gavin Bolton and David Hornbrook that will give a more rounded view of their ideas.

 ACTIVITY 1.5

Examining the main theoretical perspectives (Part A)

As you read Appendix II, consider the following questions as they apply to each quotation:

1   What is the role of the class teacher?
2   What are the children expected to 'do'?
3   How are the children's own ideas and contributions used?

4   What would the final stage of the drama lesson look like? Is there any tangible difference between them?

Also included in Appendix II are two more extracts, from Brian Way and from Betty-Jane Wagner on Dorothy Heathcote. Careful study of the books from which these extracts are taken makes useful reading for while there are idiosyncrasies of both thought and expression and the earlier works particularly speak very much with the voice of their time, much of what they say cannot be disputed. In addition there is little doubt that the writers were (and in some cases still are) inspirational teachers who fired their followers with an enthusiasm for drama which they in their turn passed on to many thousands of children.

 ACTIVITY 1.6

Examining the main theoretical perspectives (Part B)

Look back once again at the Bullying dramas and consider Questions 1–3 from Activity 1.5 above. Try to pick out specific examples. Because the dramas are described in outline with some of the detail missing, it should be possible in answering the questions to fill in some of the detail. In doing so you will be beginning to think in the way that successful teachers of drama think.

Returning to our five practitioners, in order to establish a curriculum for drama, rather than simply add one more methodology of our own invention to the growing pile, it will be more useful to examine what fundamental points they all agree upon and start from there.

DRAMA IS ALLIED TO PLAY

The point that drama is allied to play is made explicit by Peter Slade in the chosen extract but it is a fundamental point and one with which the others would have little difficulty. Since the appearance of Huizinga's *Homo Ludens* (1970), the notion of play as a cultural phenomenon has been taken seriously:

 an activity which proceeds within certain limits of time and space, in a visible order, according to rules freely accepted and outside the sphere of necessity or material utility. The play mood is one of rapture and enthusiasm and is sacred or festive in accordance with the occasion.

(p. 10)

We can readily see how this applies to all forms of drama and, of course, the manifestations of it are particularly clear when we view the activities of young children. We shall be dealing with this at greater length in the next Unit but what is relevant to us at this point in our quest for a coherent drama curriculum is the role of the teacher.

THE ROLE OF THE TEACHER

You have already considered the role of the teacher briefly with respect to the Bullying dramas and we will be referring back to them with specific illustrations shortly. Before we do this, however, let us say that while the teacher's part in any subject on the curriculum is taken seriously and with most subjects is relatively clear-cut, when we look at drama, especially in relation to play, confusions arise and definitions blur. This can plainly be seen in our chosen extracts. All the practitioners (even Peter Slade whose work seems to be nearest to pure play) advocate some sort of teacher intervention. But here a difficulty arises because in many cases it is not clear what form it should take. All appear to agree that the teacher should somehow be in control and that she or he should at least be guiding the children in some way. In other words letting them play by themselves unhindered by any form of adult input is not enough. Furthermore, all seem to agree that the teacher's role is to provide either a depth of experience or understanding (or both) which the children themselves would not be capable of achieving by themselves.

Here then is a significant point. As we have said elsewhere (Kitson and Spiby 1995), left to their own devices, children will create a narrative, usually with one event rapidly succeeding another. Something happens and then something else happens and then something else – and so on. What they will *not* do easily is to slow the narrative down in order to explore a situation or an issue or a character. But this is what all drama does, except perhaps the most shallow of 'action' movies. If we look at any drama from *Eastenders* to Ibsen we will see that most of the time is spent by people examining problems, talking about issues, pondering possible outcomes. As Dorothy Heathcote says in the film *Three Looms Waiting*, 'drama is a man in a mess'. The narrative is essential because it keeps our interest (we want to know what will happen) but it is only a part of the drama, and frequently a minor part.

Looking back to the Bullying dramas we see that in all three cases the teachers Chris, Derek and Terri are at the very heart of the process and that the techniques they use are almost all to do with this process of slowing down the drama. When Chris sets up the chair in the middle of the circle for the statementing exercise the children are engaged in exploring the character of Jason, deciding what people both closely involved and distantly acquainted think of him. Left to their own devices they would probably have gone straight for a bullying episode – and given the current obsession with violence in films and on television it would undoubtedly have been much concerned with blood and gore! An even clearer example is Terri's use of forum theatre where every line of improvised dialogue is held up to scrutiny in order that it should be conveying what the class wants it to convey. Remember the 'class' includes Terri who has at least an equal say in what goes on.

Another point that you will have noticed many times in your work with children is that left to themselves they will provide 'magic' solutions to problems that arise in the course of their play. If a key is needed to unlock the door of the dungeon, a child will miraculously 'find' one. If they are hungry and need food, a banquet will suddenly be discovered. If a particular skill is required, be it carpentry, burglary or sky-diving, someone will be able to do it. There is no consideration of probability (or to use the technical term, verisimilitude); whatever is needed to further the narrative is simply conjured up to supply that need. Now we all know from our film/television/theatre watching that such magic solutions make for very boring drama. Difficulties must be overcome through striving. There must be a struggle with a real threat of failure in order to make it exciting and interesting. And it is here once again that the role of the teacher in terms of intervention is a vital one. The teacher can prevent the magic solution and create in its place the struggle which in turn will lead to the engrossing quality that characterizes good drama. That is why both Chris and Terri's dramas end well. The magic solution would be that Andrew and Jason shake hands and live happily ever after in peace and harmony. But although that might bring some temporary instant gratification, ultimately it would be dissatisfying. Problems are not so easily solved – and such learning is a vital part of growing up.

In subsequent Units we will be discussing the practical ways in which we can achieve the right quality (and quantity) of teacher intervention, but our discussion has already led us on to the fundamental question of what exactly drama is.

KEY POINTS

Teacher intervention in drama is crucial:

a)   It slows the drama down.
b)   It stops 'magic solutions'.

THE NATURE OF DRAMA

All the practitioners we have cited would agree on one thing at least: at its most basic level, drama involves a story of some kind. It is in the nature of the story, in its purpose and in the form that it takes that the disagreement arises. In the past few years, however, a great deal of thought has been given to and a considerable amount of work done on examining the fundamental nature of drama and this may help to cut through the Gordian knot of apparently irreconcilable differences.

The Polish theatre director Jerzy Grotowski (1969) almost thirty years ago reduced drama down to three basic elements: an actor in a space with an audience watching. More recently, the distinguished critic and commentator Martin Esslin (1987) has expanded the definition into:

mimetic action, in the sense of the re-enactment of 'real' or fictional events, involving the action and interaction of human beings, real or simulated (e.g. puppets or cartoon characters) before an audience as though they were happening at that very moment.

He goes on to say that the audience is an essential ingredient:

> Even a rehearsal has an audience: the director, or, indeed, the actors themselves, who are observing the evolution and effectiveness of their own performance, in order to shape or improve it further.
>
> (p. 28)

This then provides an answer to the dogma, frequently stated, which denies that drama-in-education has anything to do with 'performance' or 'audiences'. It also shows us clearly another difference between 'drama' and 'play'. An activity in drama is one that assumes the presence of an audience even if the audience consists of just the actors themselves, or even more remotely, if the audience is only a shadowy possibility. Contrast this with play where the participants exhibit a quite different quality: that of self absorption where there is little awareness of anything outside the world they have created. The difficulty of considering this, of course, is that the two states of play and drama are frequently very close together, particularly with young children, but intervention by the teacher can be used to move them from one to another. For example if a teacher moves into a pretend corner where play activities are going on, by adopting the role of say, a worried neighbour, the teacher causes the children to move into drama mode partly because the teacher is not a child (one of them) but also because the teacher provides the audience quality absent in free play. The teacher will also, as we outlined in the previous section, pose problems and block magic solutions in order to move the activity further into drama. Why the teacher should wish to do so, we will consider in the next Unit.

ACTIVITY 1.7

Actor/audience relationship

In the following episodes consider the actor/audience relationship. In each episode, who (if any) is the audience? What is the audience in each episode expected to 'do' – participate? overhear? react in some way? be a witness so that they can do something later with what they have heard and seen? etc.

1   Terri taking the role of a worried parent on the telephone.
2   Terri taking the role of Jason and being 'hot-seated' by the class.
3   Children in Derek's class performing still images to the rest of the class.
4   Terri in the role of Andrew performing a monologue.
5   Derek's staff meeting with the teachers of Jason and Andrew's school.
6   Terri's forum theatre of a scene between Jason, Andrew and witnesses to the bullying.

The idea that, at its very heart, drama is performance goes a great way to solving some of the problems that have beset the theories of drama-in-education over the years. Firstly it enables all those apparently disparate manifestations discussed earlier not just to be brought together under one umbrella but to be seen philosophically as essentially the same. The Assembly play and the drama exercise, the role play and the drama game can all be viewed from the same perspective. Even play texts, if they are seen as 'blueprints for performance' as is now standard practice in the English and drama departments of colleges and universities, take on a dynamic, living quality rather than just words on a page.

We understand that one of the difficulties in accepting this view is the erroneous idea that performance by children is by its nature undesirable; either shallow or precocious. We have all seen children barking learned lines at an audience or performing a grotesque mimicry of adult behaviour. Nevertheless, it does not have to be like this; children *can* perform with an inner conviction that makes the drama good and worthwhile. The answer lies in the quality of the experience they undergo.

KEY POINTS

Drama involves a story.

The basic ingredients are an actor in a space with an audience.

All drama involves an audience.

All drama involves performance.

THE DRAMA EXPERIENCE

We can perhaps find a key to understanding the drama experience if we consider how in the professional theatre actors tackle the problem of assuming a role. In the majority of cases what happens is that they are presented with a script containing the words their characters are to speak, together with some stage directions about what they do in the course of the play. During the process of rehearsal they then attempt to 'get inside' their part, to make the character somehow 'real', to allow the words they speak and the feelings they portray to appear genuine. How this process occurs has been the subject of many studies and a great deal of speculation. The actors often can't describe exactly what happens and each one has his or her own method of getting to grips with it. These can seem frustratingly vague to an outsider: one famous actress claims that she does it through wearing the right shoes for the character, another describes the process as mixing and baking her part in an oven (Brook 1990). But what seems to happen is that they transfer from a *cognitive* to an *affective* state. In other words, they start by reading the words on the page and *understanding* them with that part of the brain that deals with such processes. At this stage they often engage in research to develop the understanding which might involve studying a historical period if the play is set in the past, or reading a literary analysis of the play if it is part of the classical repertoire. They are able to discuss their character, look at the motives that drive him or her and speculate on how he or she might react in this or that circumstance. They will probably *sympathize* with the character's plight and understand why the character acts as he or she does. By the time the rehearsal period is over, however, this will have changed. The understanding and sympathy will still be there but the actors will have something more. They will *identify* with the character, will have created for themselves the *feelings* that motivate the action and *empathize* with his or her behaviour. It has often been said that an actor learns to 'live' the character and although this can be misinterpreted, it does give the right impression of the affective state the actor has reached during performance.

Clearly this is a simplified model; the whole area of cognitive/affective states is highly contentious and open to widely differing interpretations. For example, Best (1992) casts doubt on the notion that they are separate states while Dryden and Voss (1994) and Goleman (1995) support the notion that each belongs to a different side of the brain. For our purposes, however, the model is useful because the idea of cognitive and affective learning casts light on what happens during a drama experience.

There is a crucial difference, however, between the professional theatre and drama-in-education. As we have indicated, the process of moving from a cognitive to an affective state in the way that professional actors do is very difficult and is not only beyond children but also beyond most adults. Herein lies the problem with children 'performing' in the way indicated above. Starting from a script and learning the words, they often simply can't reach the affective state where emotional behaviour can be portrayed in a genuine and truthful manner. They resort instead to *imitating* either what they think such behaviour should look like or what someone has coached them to do. The effect usually looks false but often it is also wooden, exaggerated, stereotypical, or a combination of all three.

More important from our point of view, however, is that drama lessons that start cognitively and then attempt to move to an affective position are frequently condemned to failure.

KEY POINTS

Professional actors working with scripts work from the cognitive to the affective. This is very difficult and takes great skill.

With children we need to start with the affective and then move to the cognitive. It's what makes drama work.

In order to appreciate just how difficult the move from cognitive to affective is, try the following exercise. If you can, work with other people, but it is possible to do it alone.

ACTIVITY: 1.8

Moving from cognitive to affective (Part A)

Imagine you are villagers who have lived for generations in the same village. The time is the eighteenth century. You have just been told by the landowner (who doesn't appear in this scene) that you are going to have to move because the village is going to be demolished in order for a canal to be built. You don't know where you are going to be moved to or indeed if the landowner is going to provide you with alternative accommodation.

If you are working in a group, discuss the news and try to *create* the feelings for yourselves that would be associated with such news: apprehension, fear, sadness, etc. If you are working on your own, try to create the feelings by just thinking about them.

We've just tried this exercise and found it impossible to do. We couldn't make the jump just *thinking* about what it would be like to be *feeling* it. It seemed as if we needed more input somehow to get us into it. Maybe if we had an emotional speech written by a good playwright, we'd be more successful.

 ACTIVITY 1.9

Moving from cognitive to affective (Part B)

Try the following short speech from *Death of a Salesman* by Arthur Miller. Willy, the salesman of the title has committed suicide because he considers himself to be a failure. His wife Linda says these words at his graveside. As you speak the words, try to create the feelings of grief that Linda experiences.

 Forgive me, dear. I can't cry. I don't know what it is, but I can't cry. I don't understand it. Why did you ever do that? Help me Willy, I can't cry. It seems to me that you're just on another trip. Why did you do it. I search and search and I search and I can't understand it, Willy. I made the last payment on the house today. Today, dear. And there'll be nobody home. [*A sob rises in her throat.*] We're free and clear. [*sobbing more fully, released*] We're free. We're free...We're free...

Once again, it wasn't very successful when we tried it. We found we could *appreciate* the emotions of grief that Linda was experiencing but when we came to speak them, all sorts of things got in the way. Like the first exercise, we needed more input and more time.

MOVING FROM AFFECTIVE TO COGNITIVE

We suspect that like us, for most people these activities will have proved to be beyond them mainly because the processes involved are both complex and introspective. You will probably have been able to *understand* the feelings but not actually to feel them for yourselves, except perhaps dimly. In order to do it we have to rely either on what has been termed 'emotional memory' (Stanislavsky 1950) or a subtle ability to create all the requisite feelings and emotions simply out of an imaginative response to what it would be like if it really were happening to us.

On the other hand, and this is a vital point, if we do it the other way around and move instead from an affective state to a cognitive one, we find that the process is much easier and one with which we are familiar. We only have to think of a film, a play or a television programme that has moved us (an affective response) to realize how quickly we progress to thinking about it, discussing it with friends, pondering on the outcomes, etc. (a cognitive response). This tends to happen when we are members of an audience but it is even more powerful when we are actually involved in the dramatic experience. It seems that making sense of this experience by submitting it to questioning, reason and logic seems also to be a natural corollary (see Best 1985). Certainly, even the most recalcitrant child who has experienced something in drama will require very little encouragement to talk about it, reflect upon it, learn from it. And this has been one of the strongest arguments advanced by teachers of drama for retaining its place on the curriculum.

Naturally, the problem that faces every such teacher is how actually to create an experience for the children that will produce the affective response we have been talking about, especially as so much of our curriculum in school is concerned directly with learning by cognitive means. While the concern of this book is to demonstrate effective ways by which this might be achieved, the highlighting of the affective/cognitive dialectic does show us that drama encompasses a number of different types of learning, all of which are integral to drama as a form of art.

For example, the personal development that Brian Way emphasized in his teaching can be attributed to the affective state where such qualities as empathy, working together harmoniously and being sensitive to the needs of others in the group are all stressed. On the other hand, the fact that in a Gavin Bolton lesson children may have learned a great deal about the Saxon way of life in a drama about a Saxon village is firmly located in the cognitive domain. A recognition that the two exist together is important not only because of what it offers to the children in terms of a learning experience but because it goes a great deal of the way to appreciating just how drama can also be regarded as an art form in its own right.

It might seem at this point that we are claiming that drama is the only subject where the affective and cognitive states interplay – and of course this is plainly nonsense. We have all seen children emotionally engaged with a piece of literature, a story from history, a science experiment or the solving of a maths puzzle; and from this emotional engagement come shifts of understanding. We are advancing the view that one of the uses of drama is as a tool in this process and one that can create not only a powerful experience but an enhanced understanding of the issues involved in the particular subject area. We will be demonstrating how this can occur in the drama and science lesson in the next Unit.

KEY POINTS

If we have an affective experience, it is easy to apply cognitive processes to make sense of it.

The same applies to children.

The combination of affective and cognitive is one of the things that gives drama its power.

FORM AND CONTENT

Apart from the reconciliation of both cognitive and affective experience as part of drama another difficulty in appreciating the subject as an art form has been in the notion of form and content. It is as if each of the sides in the 'art-form' quarrel have taken one of these aspects to themselves (either form or content) and accused their opponents of down-grading the other. So to those who have not read his writings carefully, it might seem that Gavin Bolton is in favour of the drama experience, both cognitive and affective, while at the same time ignoring the form that surrounds it, particularly when that form embraces overtly theatrical elements such as lighting, costume and performance before an audience. Similarly, to those who have only skim-read David Hornbrook he appears to advocate all those aspects associated with theatre form while failing to give proper value to the experience itself.

All this has a bearing on our consideration of a curriculum for drama because if we are to teach it properly we must offer learning both of content and form to our pupils. We see how absurd one is without the other if we consider other arts subjects such as music, dance, or fine art itself. Letting children splash around with paint for a while might be enjoyable, it might even be therapeutic and may well be necessary to begin with but after a while the enjoyment and the learning comes about through grappling with and mastering the form itself. The learning of technique is a powerful weapon in this process. On the other hand, few people would wish to return to the kind of art curriculum where rules of perspective, say, have to be learned before children are allowed to paint a picture.

Closer to home as far as drama is concerned, and linked directly to the English part of the National Curriculum is the process by which children learn about storytelling. At first they take delight in simply hearing, telling and writing stories for themselves. Gradually, however, they learn about story-form, about the techniques of building tension, making a good ending and so forth. In that way they learn both to use and to manipulate the form for themselves and to appreciate the use of it in the stories of others. In the same way, children will at first enjoy the experience of taking part in a drama with the teacher and be content to reflect afterwards simply on 'what happened'. Fairly soon, however, the teacher will begin to teach them ways in which the drama can be structured so that together they can make it work effectively. From there, they learn how elements of theatre can be used to further enhance their work.

If we consider that for GCSE drama the final assessment almost invariably requires students to be able to construct and enact effective dramas for themselves, we can see that at primary level we are laying down the foundations for this to happen. In drama, perhaps more than any subject, it is tempting for we teachers to keep the 'mysteries' of the subject to ourselves, often for the very laudable reason that by doing so we will be in a position to spring dramatic surprises, build electrifying climaxes, introduce awe-inspiring music at the critical moment, and so on.

We will see later in the book that this idea is often a mistaken one, and that if the children know about such things in advance it does not necessarily lessen their impact but rather enhances it. The process of the drama curriculum should be one of increasing empowerment for the participants.

KEY POINT

Drama works most successfully when children are not only dealing with the content but also have learned how to manipulate the form.

Drama can highlight issues for children and through working in this way the teacher is able to present complex dilemmas in the children's own language. The work need not be the most effective dramatic presentation ever performed so long as it is able to breathe life into history, geography, science or maths. As we discuss in later chapters teachers like Terri, Chris and Derek are not in the business of allowing the children to create 'magic solutions'. Teachers must deal honestly and sensitively with the children's introduction of facts and inconsistencies into the narrative. It is the teacher's responsibility to judge when to correct or discuss outside of the story something that a child has said. Drama is a powerful method of working and as such needs to be part of the wider range of teaching strategies available to all teachers.

  ACTIVITY 1.10

A curriculum defined

Before moving on to the next Unit which will deal with the learning process involved in drama, we will look at the drama criteria provided by the Office for Standards in Education (OFSTED) as a guide for its inspectors. Although its method of assessment has since been revised, quite clearly this is what it was looking for within the drama curriculum when it conducted an inspection in schools.

Begin by reading the following extract taken from the OFSTED Inspectors handbook (Inspection Schedule: Guidance).

Standards should be judged in the following aspects of pupils' achievements: using imagination, with belief and feeling; creating drama with conviction and concentration; responding sensitively to their own work and that of others in drama; using a range of dramatic skills, techniques, forms and conventions to express ideas and feeling; effectively grasping and using dramatic concepts appropriately; recalling, recording and evaluating their own work and that of others.

Now relate this to the drama that takes place in your own school. The following questions may be useful:

- Do the children have opportunities to use their imagination?
- How far does the work involve building belief and feeling, concentration and conviction?
- Do the children have the opportunity to use a range of dramatic skills?
- Do they have access to different forms and conventions to express their ideas?
- How are they encouraged to evaluate their own work and that of others?

ANSWERS AND SUGGESTIONS

Activity 1.1 The nature of school drama

Some suggestions of activities that take place in school under the name of drama: role play; simulations; war-games; charades; improvisation; making up plays in groups; assembly plays; nativity plays; school play; playing in the Wendy House; dressing up; puppetry; making and wearing masks; acting out stories; whole-group drama with the teacher playing a role as well; music and movement; 'being trees'; drama on the radio; dance drama; poetry reading; choral speaking; drama games.

Activity 1.4 Identifying attitudes and viewpoints

We have identified the teachers in the extract with some of the ideas of the following practitioners:

Teacher One   David Hornbrook
Teacher Two   Peter Slade
Teacher Three   Gavin Bolton

Unit 2

Learning through drama

Whilst the theorists of educational drama that we met in Unit 1 might differ as to the exact nature of the learning that takes place when children are engaged in the drama process, they do all agree that in drama many different types of learning are possible. As we have pointed out, drama is an ephemeral subject. There are few things to photograph and little to record and all that remains at the end of a session are the feelings that were created and the changes in understanding that the drama has brought about. With nothing to look at and nothing to hold, it is no wonder then that teachers unused to this way of working find it hard to capitalize on the true potential of drama and the unique learning opportunities that it creates. In this Unit we will look firstly at how the learning process works within the drama and then examine how teachers can stimulate and extend this learning. As we go through it we will be returning to the classrooms of Terri, Chris and Derek to follow their lessons and to look at how they are able to draw the learning opportunities out of the drama lessons they teach. Before we do that though, try the following:

 ACTIVITY 2:1

Learning areas [Part A]

Cast your minds back to the bullying dramas. Clearly there was a great deal for the children to learn in relation to personal and social education as well as learning about how the drama was actually used and developed.

Consider Terri's lesson for a moment. Brainstorm a list of learning areas that were opened up by the drama. These were not areas that were fully developed because time wouldn't allow for it. They were created by the drama and had the potential to be further developed by Terri if she had wished.

> When you've done this look at the list that you have created and see what grouping of learning areas emerges.

Let us return to the classroom of Chris Johnson. She has been looking at environmental issues in science and felt that this could be taught through drama.

The work has been planned as part of the work on conservation that the children have been engaged in for a number of weeks. The focus for Chris is to encourage the children to move beyond the 'magic solutions' frequently found in their own play, to attempt to solve problems and get them to face up to the results of their decision making.

At the start of the drama Chris puts the children into role as researchers in a company making fertilizers. The company has been very successful and has moved to a new plant by the coast. She asks the children to think what their research might involve and what equipment they might be using in the laboratory. Chris herself takes on the role of senior researcher. She has taken on this role as she feels that it will enable her to encourage and direct the children by asking questions about their work, thus keeping them on task. The group begins its work. The children fiddle with imaginary microscopes and tend pretend plants, some working in small groups and others working on their own.

During this part of the work the researchers are told by Chris to stop work and are informed of a problem that has just arisen. A crack in the disposal pipe from the factory has

Plate 1 Children create a still image of scientists working

just been discovered. In her role as the senior researcher she tells them that despite this they should carry on with their work and dispose of the waste in the normal manner by putting it down the 'disposal pipe'. The end of the day is reached, the experiments cleared away and the waste disposed of down the pipe as normal.

Just before leaving the laboratory Chris calls them all together. She tells them that she has some news from the senior management of the factory. She then reads them a letter which tells them how well they are doing and that they might well be included in the new profit-share bonus scheme. This would mean a lot more money for all of them and it would also mean that their jobs would be more secure.

Out of role the children are encouraged to reflect on the story so far. Chris asks them to think about some simple questions.

- Who are they?
- What has happened?
- What might be going to happen next?

She does this so that she can fix the story in their minds and that any uncertainties can be sorted out. She finds that this is a good way of working as it means that the children are all working on the same story rather than working on lots of different ones.

When she has done this Chris tells them that they are going to meet someone else in the story and that what they are to do is just listen to what is being said. With the children sitting around her on the floor she begins to speak the thoughts of a mussel farmer who works on the coast near to the factory. There is no sense of 'acting' but there is a real sense of listening to the words of 'another person' here in the room with us.

Chris likes this ways of working. She finds that both she and the children are comfortable with it and that she can convey a great deal of information quickly. It has a dramatic quality that holds the class's interest. She has already worked out some broad details of the character she is pretending to be in the story. Pulling an old shawl around her shoulders, she takes on the role of the mussel farmer. The prop of the shawl isn't essential but she finds that it helps both her and the children believe just that little bit more. It just seems to make things work more effectively.

Having got across the biographical details in this way Chris begins to tell the story of how the mussels are collected by hand by her and her husband. They're then placed onto the tractor before being taken up to the shed to be cleaned and sorted. Her father had used a horse and cart but apart from that the job has been the same for generations. The work is hard and it is often cold here on the coast. Despite being the family trade they had had to give up all the mussel beds a few years ago because of the pollution from the towns along the coast. Recently the coast has been cleaned up and mussels have come back. They have worked hard to re-establish the beds and it is a good living again, especially now with the trading in Europe. They can sell straight to Spain. They had borrowed money from the bank for a new cleaning plant and newer tractor. The crop is better than ever now, the mussels are bigger than they used to be and much tastier. She doesn't know why but feels it might be something to do with the new chemical factory a little way up the coast.

Chris stops at this point. The whole speech hasn't lasted for more than four or five minutes and the children have listened intently. She then splits the class into smaller groups and they are asked to begin to write down what they know of the mussel farmer. They are

Plate 2 Using a shawl the teacher creates the role of the mussel farmer

able to come up with a great deal of information based on what they have just heard and then go on to think of questions that they could ask her to find out more about her and the mussel farmers' way of life. They come up with a whole host of things to ask.

With the children again sitting in front of her, Chris puts on the shawl and once more goes into role as the farmer. This time instead of just listening to the thoughts the class are told to ask their questions which she then answers.

Chris can clearly remember the first time she tried this way of working, having seen it used when she was at college. It had looked so easy, but on her own, she had felt terrified of not being able to come up with the 'right' answers to their questions. Despite her initial fears she now finds that she is able to give very plausible responses to what they ask with only the slightest creative elaboration!

At this point she stops the work. Having introduced the farmer she is now going to ask the children to return to being the researchers in the factory because she wants to introduce a dilemma into the drama. This is the main learning point that the lesson has been set up to address.

With the children once more in the role of the researchers they are called together at the factory by the senior researcher. She has just received information from the European Union's Commission on coastal water standards. (Chris doesn't know if it exists but it sounds good!) They have done tests in the coastal region by the factory and found that there are high degrees of chemicals in the sea, very similar to those that have been found in samples of shellfish, especially mussels, imported from this region into Spain.

In order to make the link between the two ends of the story Chris mentions the local mussel farmers and how she has heard that they might have to stop production because of the toxins in the shellfish.

Chris now has done her bit. She has put all the pieces of the jigsaw together and all that is left is for the children to sort it out. It is at this point that she withdraws and hands over the drama to the children . It is they who have to decide what should be done. Clearly their factory is causing the pollution but the high rates of fertilizers being put into the sea are also causing the local mussel beds to flourish, thus helping farmers. The dilemma that they have to resolve is, should they stop discharging the effluent into the sea? If they do, it would slow down production and seriously effect their promised bonuses as well as putting the local mussel farmers out of business again. If they don't, the increased toxins in the shellfish might affect people's health – and who knows what other undiscovered problems this pollution might be causing. They would get the bonuses, however, and the mussel farmers would continue to prosper.

The children do not find this an easy decision to make. They work in small groups and have only five minutes to come up with a solution. They consider the morality of covering up the truth in some way. They consider the importance of the product that they are making to a large number of farmers and the people who eat what they grow. They think abut the mussel farmers and their livelihood – and the people who eat their product. The groups then present their thoughts to the rest of the class. After lively discussion, the decision is made to clean up the discharge of fertilizers going into the sea at the same time recognizing that as a by-product of this action they will seriously affect the newly flourishing mussel trade.

The final section of the drama is a meeting between the researchers and Chris in role as the mussel farmer. She is told that the leaking of the fertilizers into the sea had made their crop so successful and also that the company has decided to install extra filters in order to prevent the leakage. The children then have to explain that this will certainly result in a drop in production of mussels and the probable loss of her livelihood. She doesn't make it easy for them!

As you can see from this lesson there was much more going on than simply 'going through a story'. There were a number of learning opportunities that Chris was trying to exploit over and above getting the children to work in groups and getting them to understand something about the drama process.

So then, what kind of things were the children learning?

    ACTIVITY 2.2

Learning areas [Part B]

Following the line of the story, list what you feel were the learning areas that Chris and the class touched on. Some will be knowledge-based (to do with pollution), some will be skills-based (to do with ways of working) and some will be related to cognitive development (moral problem solving). If there are several of you working together you can either work in small groups and share your ideas or work as one large group. When you have done that decide which of the areas of learning were focus areas (the main ones) and which were incidental.

Firstly it can be seen that the lesson not only stretched the children in terms of understanding the moral dimensions of responsibility but also forced them to use a variety of linguistic registers and structure arguments. The issue of pollution actually benefiting someone was a real surprise for them and needed a considerable cognitive reorganization. Above all this simple story made them aware that the issues of pollution and conservation are not always as clear-cut as they imagine. Throughout the lesson the children were motivated and on task and they felt that they had made up a good story. What they were less aware of was the fact that they had been tackling complex issues, using discussion and debating skills, and working effectively in a variety of different group structures as well as finding out more about themselves and how they feel.

Derek worked in a very different way in his drama on pollution. He set up a situation where the children were faced with the problem of a cement factory that had been failing to keep control of the dust that was escaping into the atmosphere. He found the basic idea for the story in the local paper and had saved the cutting. He set the group up as the local residents who had just found out about the increase in pollution and showed them the article. He asked them to discuss what they should do about it. In the public meeting that followed the children came up with two of the 'magic solutions' that were mentioned in Unit 1. One of the boys announced to the meeting that he was a scientist and he'd invented a machine that would clean up the pollution; another of the class suggested that the factory was closing down anyway and that they were going to start to make clothes there now. Derek not being part of the drama but rather on the edge of what was going on found it very difficult to intervene as the children moved away from the learning area of pollution. He went along with their ideas as he had seen Dorothy Heathcote do in the video that he'd once seen and they talked about how they should be in the factory and what they should make. Again he watched rather helplessly as one group of girls practised being models for the clothes whilst some other children set to work building a new machine. He had suggested that the new machine might be used for recycling the scrap cloth but they said it was for cutting out new clothes.

ACTIVITY 2.3

The role of the teacher

Clearly the learning focus of Derek's drama has shifted. What do you think his original focus for the learning might have been? Quickly jot it down.

Now compare this with what actually happened. At what point do the two plans diverge? What difference do you think would have occurred if he had taken the following courses of action?

- Gone into role as a unemployed worker.
- Chaired the meeting.
- Got the children to be factory workers.
- Started the drama some time before the discovery of the pollution.
- Set up a meeting between the factory workers and the locals.

Clearly if we look at Chris's drama and then look at Derek's there is a difference in the learning outcomes for the children. But how do the children actually learn through the drama process?

In order to examine this we need to consider what we feel is the very root of the drama process – that is, we need briefly to look at children's play. As we mentioned in the previous Unit, drama at its simplest is just an extension of fantasy play. If you have ever watched young children playing you will have seen the way that they experiment and test out their ideas. As children learn through playing with objects so they learn through make-believe fantasy play, out of which we as teachers develop the drama process.

FANTASY PLAY AND ITS RELATIONSHIP TO DRAMA

It might at first glance seem rather strange to start with an exploration of fantasy play but the importance of fantasy play or drama and its role in child development has been supported by a wide spectrum of writers ranging from Freud (1959) and Piaget (1952) to Winnicot (1971), Singer and Singer (1990) and Smilansky (1990). This has been interpreted by some practitioners as meaning that one should leave children uninterrupted to explore their fantasy worlds in drama and within their own horizons – clearly the thinking behind Derek's drama in the example above. Working on their own in this way children will frequently repeat the same form of play, enact the same type of stories in their drama, engage in the same role activity, model the same type of behaviour and resolve similar problems. One would not be surprised to find Derek's class acting out the types of problems with similar solutions whether looking at a drama on pollution or looking at the problem of press freedom. Effective intervention by the teacher can channel this learning, construct new dilemmas and challenges, encourage and support individuals and extend and motivate language use. Clearly this was operating in Chris's lesson whilst the lack of intervention hampered Derek's drama. Through such sensitive intervention we can help children to operate way above their normal level. In this manner we are able to help the child engage in work 'as though he were a head taller than himself' (Vygotsky 1978: 102). We will now look at this in more detail by examining the nature of drama and the theoretical implications that underpin it, to explore the ways in which the teacher can help the children get the most out of the learning situation that is created by the drama.

LEARNING THROUGH PLAYING

Even at Key Stage 2 the children in your class will engage in a wide variety of play activities and the element of fantasy will occur at differing levels within individual 'games' and at different levels of maturity. Let's put the development of play into drama and the associated development of learning into a continuum so that we can see how the children benefit from the activity.

Socio-dramatic play (of which drama is an extension) is for the most part concerned with the nature of role and of social interaction whilst other types of play involve bodily activity or the use and exploration of objects. There are four main types of play according to Bruce (1991): functional play, constructive play, rule-governed play and socio-dramatic play:

- *Functional play*
  Here children explore their sensory motor activities, repeating and modifying actions that are part of their natural activities. The repetition and control are found to be pleasurable so that the whole exercise can be repeated at a later date. Through functional play children learn about their physical capabilities and their effect on the environment.
- *Constructive play*
  In this play children see themselves as creators. The activity is again sensory motor but this time there is the addition of a plan and the child begins to organize materials and objects in accordance with this plan. Often the activity is engaged in for the sense of enjoyment of creation and it is characterized by the fact that often something is left behind.
- *Game with rules*
  Smilansky (1990) subdivides this type of play into two categories, table games and physical games. Both require the child to agree to a proscribed set of rules controlling reactions and actions within specific limits.
- *Dramatic and socio-dramatic play*
  This type of play demonstrates children's growing awareness of their social surroundings and can be observed from an early age developing in parallel to other play behaviour. Here the child consciously acts out social interaction and by so doing can experience human relationships actively by means of symbolic representation (Smilansky 1990).

 ACTIVITY 2.4

Imaginative play

Read the following quotation from Singer and Singer:

 Imaginative play is fun, but in the midst of the joys of making believe, children may also be preparing for the reality of more effective lives.
Singer and Singer (1990: 152)

Think back to Chris's lesson on pollution. In what ways were the children preparing for adult life and to what extent were they engaged in a play activity? How does this differ from what occurred in Derek's class?

WHY IS SUCH ACTIVITY SO IMPORTANT?

At a time of increased pressure upon curriculum time, teachers are constantly exploring ways in which they can fit more into the day and certainly the idea of children at Key Stage 2 playing must be regarded with suspicion. Yet there is much evidence to show the value of drama activities and we will examine some of this here.

Although it is a crude distinction, theories relating to drama can be viewed in terms of psycho-analytic theory as exemplified by Freud and of cognitive processing theory suggested by Piaget – to which we can add the more functionalist views put forward by Bruner. Irrespective of their differing opinions regarding the contribution to child development all stress the importance of fantasy play and advocate its inclusion in the ongoing education of individuals.

Freud saw fantasy as a way to gain access to the psyche. Emphasizing the function of the child's instincts in fantasy play he suggested that through play children will show their inner selves. This play becomes like a mirror to the child's subconscious and as such it can be used as a diagnostic and therapeutic tool. Within the dramatic context, the children construct roles by projecting on to them imaginative and emotional components. Acting out these roles through drama helps the child by weakening the effect of the emotional pressure and by so doing helps her or him to assimilate the traumatic experience. This is the process Freud refers to as sublimation.

Piaget further looks at fantasy play, and by extension drama, in terms of assimilation and accommodation. He sets up the theoretical notion of a schema (a collection of associated ideas) to which new ideas and new relationships of existing ideas are joined on. This process he calls assimilation. He suggests that in fantasy play (drama) the fantasy elements can be assimilated into a particular schema. Even though it is fantasy the assimilation process occurs as if it were happening in real life. If in the drama the children are making up a story about going on a journey then they draw upon their existing knowledge of journeys (their existing schemas) and add any new information that they get through the play. In Chris's drama at the start of this Unit the children were making up a story about researchers. They have never been scientists but they do have odd pieces of information about such a role that they may have picked up from the media, from school, or other forms of cultural transmission. If, however, the new information is completely novel and there is no existing schema to incorporate it into, or if it actually contradicts the existing schema, then this must be accommodated in order that the new information may fit. As a result new inter-connections will be made. The drama being a form of fantasy play can help children test out ideas and concepts and by so doing make sense of them through assimilation and accommodation. We can see this in action as they try to work out what should be done to curb the pollution and how this might affect the livelihood of the local mussel farmers.

Through the drama they create new pretend situations which can contain within them a wide range of seemingly unconnected elements all drawn from their previous experiences. The fantasy acts as a way of unifying the experiences, knowledge and understanding, thus helping them to discover the links between the individual components. Moreover, as the children are able to control the drama they are also able to control the components. Your children engaged in a 'fantasy' about a space journey will selectively combine a wide range of components about 'space' and 'journeys', such as what it is like to go on a journey, how you have to get ready, how time does not stand still whilst you are away, how it feels good to arrive and so on, with things to do with space: it is dark, it is a long way away, you need oxygen, you need special clothes, and so on. Singer and Singer (1990) argue that if this form of activity is insufficiently valued by schools and teachers then its natural potential for developing the children's understanding changes and it goes 'underground'. What is needed in the primary years is the building up of drama as a method of learning, the legitimizing of activity so that the children themselves can come to understand the value of it. As Bolton (1979) suggests it is through this that considerable learning about our lives, the way people interact, the workings of society and our role within it can take place.

Erickson (1965) stresses the importance of the life rehearsal element in fantasy play activities such as drama. He suggests that through 'play' children can begin to learn to cope with life and with a range of complex social issues such as failure, loneliness and disappointment. In his work he encouraged children to enact fantasy scenes and was surprised to discover that these scenes were metaphors of the children's lives. Bolton (1979) takes this one stage further by arguing that all drama is a metaphor for the children's lives and that it is the function of the teacher to enable the children to reflect on the significance on their play to learn from it.

 Imaginative play is fun, but in the midst of the joys of making believe, children may also be preparing for the reality of more effective lives.

Singer and Singer (1990: 152)

No doubt if you have set up dramas in your class you too will have been aware of the areas of strength that drama offers both the teacher and the children. Singer and Singer (1990) identify three significant areas where the benefits of drama can be seen:

- An increase in actual spontaneous verbal output of around 50 per cent in socio-dramatic play.
- A corresponding increase in social interaction.
- A significant improvement across a range of cognitive skills after 'training' in drama.

 We can not avoid the belief that [drama] serves important purposes in the emergence of the psychologically complex and adaptable person. Individual differences in the frequency and variety of such play seem to be associated not only with richer and more complex language but also with a greater potential for cognitive differentiation, divergent thought, impulse control, self-entertainment, emotional expressiveness and , perhaps, self awareness.

Singer and Singer (1990: 151)

Sara Smilansky (1968) ties this into the work of the classroom when she proposes a range of generalizations relating to the value of socio-dramatic play that show how such play can influence the creativity, intellectual growth and social skills of the child. Among her generalized notions of the benefits of drama are the following:

- Creating new combinations out of experiences.
- Selectivity and intellectual discipline.
- Discrimination of the central features of a role sequence.

- Heightened concentration.
- Enhanced self awareness and self control.
- Self discipline within the role context (e.g. a child who is playing a special role within a game might inhibit crying because the character in the game would not cry).
- The acquisition of flexibility and empathy towards others.
- The development of an intrinsic set of standards.
- Acquisition of a sense of creativity and capacity to control personal responses.
- Development of co-operative skills since make believe games in groups require effective give and take.
- Awareness of the potential use of the environment for planning and other play situations.
- Increased sensitivity to alternative role possibilities so that the notion of father need not be one's own father but may include many kinds of behaviour.
- Increased capacity for the development of abstract thought by learning first to substitute the image for the overt action and then later a verbal coding for both the action and the image.
- Heightened capacity for generalisation.
- A set towards vicarious learning and a greater use of modelling.

(Smilansky 1968 in Singer and Singer 1990: 224)

It would be wrong to argue that every child engaged in drama activities will automatically take on all of these functions, nor will children *not* engaged in drama fail to have these areas of learning available to them. Rather it is argued that involvement in drama provides an opportunity for the child to gain access to those elements that Smilansky identifies.

   ACTIVITY 2.5

Smilansky's list

Using the list of learning outcomes for drama set out above think back to either Chris Johnson's environmental drama at the beginning of this Unit or a drama you have seen or have taken part in. How many of the points above can you identify as being present in the drama. What else would you wish to add to the list?

INTERVENTION AND THE TEACHER'S ROLE

As we showed in the previous Unit, drama theorists and teachers have viewed their function within the process of drama in very different ways but all of them are clear that the teacher does play a significant part in the process. We have already discussed the views on this matter by practitioners such as David Hornbrook, Peter Slade, Gavin Bolton and

Dorothy Heathcote. Whichever viewpoint you adopt, what is crucial is the way that you interact and intervene with the children in the drama. Although the idea of intervention might seem intrusive what it can do is maximize the learning possibilities.

In understanding this idea of intervention we have found it very useful to consider the ideas of Vygotsky (1978). He advanced the idea that children if left to themselves operate up to a naturally determined level. If you think for a moment about the times that you have watched children 'acting out plays', for example in the playground or in the classroom on a wet playtime, the stories will have a very familiar structure which does not challenge the children in the way that Chris's drama lesson did (and Derek's did not). The single most important difference in these two drama lessons was the part the teacher played in moving the children beyond this naturally determined level. Vygotsky calls this new area of learning the 'zone of proximal development' which we can translate as 'the area of new development or new learning'.

> play creates a zone of proximal development of the child. In play the child always behaves beyond his average age above his daily behaviour; in play it is as though he were a head taller than himself.

Vygotsky (1978: 102)

In drama the child's greatest achievements are possible, achievements that tomorrow will become their basic level of real action and moral reasoning. Through skilful intervention they can be encouraged to struggle with ideas, concepts and morality. In such activities we can never fail since we are working with a fantasy. Nothing of the real world has been altered, nothing has changed. There are many ways that this might be done in the classroom and yet once the children have worked through the set problems and functioned at this higher level such strategies will become part of what Vygotsky calls 'their everyday behaviour'.

Morgan and Saxton (1987) show how this intervention in drama can become the subtle tool of the teacher working with children. You can work alongside the children within the drama keeping them on task by avoiding 'magic solutions' to the problems that they encounter, enrich and deepen the work and open up new learning areas. (Think back to the differences between Chris's and Derek's dramas.) You are able to intervene and structure the learning from within, almost unobserved by the children, a strategy that Neelands (1984) describes as 'the subtle tongue of the teacher'. This we will explore in greater detail in later Units.

LEARNING AS A GROUP

Up till now we have concentrated on the cognitive aspects of learning through drama. Before we move on to examine ways of working it is worthwhile just briefly to consider the benefits of working in groups. Drama is a group activity even if the group is separated into those performing and those watching. It is a truly collaborative activity as there is no way that drama can take place when children are on their own. Such activity might be fantasy play but it is not drama. Galton and Williamson (1992) looked at group work in primary schools and concluded that the most effective learning is achieved as Vygotsky (1978) says, when the work is truly collaborative. They put forward five main conclusions based on the

Plate 3 Children gain a great deal from working in a collaborative group in drama

general research into group work. Let's now look at these and then relate them to Chris's and Derek's lessons to see the effect of the group work.

1. When children sit in groups in the classroom they are likely to achieve more if they are encouraged to co-operate either by working toward a common shared outcome or by making an individual contribution towards a common goal .... Such groupings do seem to improve pupils' self-esteem and increase pupil motivation.

2. Groups function best when they are of mixed ability but such groups must include pupils from the highest ability group within the class.

3. Children perform in different ways according to the nature of the task – conversation is highest when children are engaged in action tasks. With abstract tasks such as debates, the interactions are less frequent though of a higher quality.

4. Problem-solving tasks with a clearly testable outcome generate a higher degree of collaboration than more open-ended tasks. Where the outcomes are less clear children will tend to go for the first solution offered.

5. For successful collaboration to take place pupils need to have a clear idea of what is expected of them. Feedback from the teacher appears to be crucial.

(Galton and Williamson 1992)

ACTIVITY 2.6

Group work

Think back now to the lessons by Chris and Derek. How are the elements of successful group work set out by Galton and Williamson reflected in the two dramas? Does the work of the two drama teachers meet the criteria of effective group work?

Galton and Williamson have in addition, put forward a series of observations of how teachers handle group work.

- When giving instructions for a given task these are usually related to the end product, therefore children are told what to do in order to complete the activity satisfactorily.
- As a result children focus on the completion of the task and not the process. They are more concerned with the getting to the end of the task rather than the quality of the solution.
- This way of working creates what they call a 'cycle of frustration' where the teacher tries to slow the children down whilst the children try to complete the tasks as quickly as possible. The cycle can only be broken if more time is spent at the start of the lesson stressing the importance of the process to be used during the task.
- Collaborative group work requires a relaxed classroom ethos where both teachers and pupils feel that their needs are recognized and cared for.

 ACTIVITY 2.7

Think back for a moment to the two dramas on pollution. They were quite different in both the way they were presented and types of teacher intervention that were used. Which of the above observations best fits the work going on in Chris's classroom and which the work in Derek's?

To summarize the points made in this Unit then, the value of drama can be seen in its therapeutic, diagnostic and cognitive developmental functions. It helps the children assimilate information into existing schemas, accommodate new information to prepare for unknown situations and to place their experience of life into a context that can be interpreted through reflection. It is something of a paradox for whilst cognitive growth is *enhanced* by fantasy/socio-dramatic play the very fact of this cognitive development will mean that the child has less *need* of the fantasy in order to find out about simple behaviour patterns and motives through observation of those immediately around them. As

Smilansky (1990) points out, the increasing influence that the child actually has on the world coupled with the decreased need to test out and explore family roles enables him or her to open up and explore new horizons. Together with development in reading, this means that children have less need to explore such elements through fantasy play. What we need to do as teachers is to move children beyond these immediate horizons. Working collaboratively in groups helps with the learning process.

We must encourage pupils to begin to look at the deeper level of role and relationships in the greater complexity of life. For this to happen, we as teachers need to challenge the children in our classes. They need to be given complex dramas with complex challenges that move them beyond what they can do by themselves and on into Vygotsky's zone of proximal development. To put it simply the children need to be stretched and extended and what better way to do this than through drama.

In the next Unit we will begin to explore the ways in which this can be achieved.

Teacher strategies

In Unit 2 we examined the potential for learning through drama and what makes it a particularly potent way of working. Having once decided that drama is a suitable method of teaching your specific subject the next stage is to think about what makes a drama, how to make it work and how to draw the children into the story. In this Unit we are going to look at a wide range of teacher strategies that can make the drama process effective. As we do this, not only your understanding of the process will be developed but also your confidence as a drama teacher.

GETTING STARTED – MAKING A CONTRACT

Terri Routhwaite has just started a piece of drama with the class that looks at the idea of the integration of one culture with another. She drew the basic idea from a book that she was reading to the class but has modified the theme so that it does not rely on the narrative of the book. The 'plot' concerns a family who move from Italy into an Italian community in Britain. They own a café which over the years has become the centre for the local Italian community. The café, once prosperous, has now fallen on hard times and it may well have to close down. The issue that she wants to explore with the children is that of 'belonging' and 'cultural assimilation'.

As this is a new class who have done little drama before Terri starts by establishing a 'contract' with them. Although this sounds rather formal all that she is doing is making explicit what is normally implicit in teaching. The children have little experience of drama and as such they are not sure of the rules. They do not know how to behave. She has found in the past that when the children are uncertain of what they are doing they will push at the boundaries of behaviour in order for them to be made clear. As she says, if you sit a class of children at desks with paper and pens in front of them they will start writing. They know what is expected of them. It's not the same in drama. When a class begins they are not sure what is going to happen. It is important to let them know what is expected of them and to define the boundaries of behaviour for them.

Let's listen to Terri as she speaks to the children:

We're going to do some drama today and I know for some of you it will be the first time that you've done drama and for others it will be very familiar. I thought it would be a good idea to spend a couple of minutes just talking about what we can expect from a drama session. So what is drama? All it really is is a story that we are going make up together. We've done stories before and sometimes we write them down and sometimes we speak them out loud and today we are going to make them up as we go along. In the story we're going to be different people. You're going to be different people and I'm going to be someone different as well. Do you think you can do that for me? [She waits] Now if we are going to work in this way there are a couple of things that we have to do. Firstly we must try to help each other out so that if in the drama you notice that someone hasn't got a partner or is stuck for an idea then it would be a good idea to ask them to join your group or to share your idea with them. The second thing that I want you to try to do is to listen to each other. Let's say that you've had lots of good ideas, it might be a good idea to let someone else say their ideas. So they're the two things that I want you to try to do. Listen to each other and help each other out and if you do that for me I'll try to make the drama as interesting and exciting as I can for you.

Plate 4 Establishing a contract

What she does now is to go round each child in the class and encourage them to agree to the 'contract'.

Derek Howes, when he teaches drama, operates in a similar way except that he has worked with the class several times before so they are beginning to know what to expect from the work. Instead of going through the contract verbally he has written it out on a piece of sugar paper that he keeps from week to week and simply reads through to remind the children. He has also customized his contract to fit the needs of working in his classroom. He has told them to keep away from the tables stacked around the edge of the classroom as they might fall, and not to rush off when the bell goes but to wait for him to round off the drama.

Chris Johnson has decided to allow the children to make up their own contract suggesting those things that would make them feel safe when doing drama. They agreed on such things as the children should not laugh at each other's work nor shout out when other people are talking.

However you choose to set it up, the important thing about the contract is that it is in place and can be referred to if you feel that the children are moving away from the type of behaviour that you feel comfortable with. You can stop the drama, talk about what has gone on and then go back into the fiction without losing momentum. You are also identifying the behaviour and not the child. It is the behaviour that is inappropriate not the child that is intrinsically bad. It can be talked about and the child's self-esteem can remain intact.

Drama is often seen as a magic carpet which when being used can cope with all manner of problems. Whilst it is true that the experienced teacher can deal with a variety of situations through the role that is being used, for those with less experience it is much better just to stop the drama when difficulties arise and talk about the problem before restarting the drama.

MARKING OUT DRAMA TIME

One thing that will make children as well as adults feel uneasy and unsafe in the drama is being confused between fantasy and reality. Children can cope very effectively with the change from one state to another as can be seen in children's fantasy play. When it is controlled by them they will establish ways of marking out when it is fantasy and when it is reality. They will say things such as 'When I sit on this chair I'll be the shopkeeper' and when the interaction has been completed they will conclude with 'All right, I'm not playing now.' What makes us all feel uneasy is the sense of not knowing whether what is going on is real or not. There are numerous stories (although no doubt many are apocryphal) of stage managers standing on theatre stages asking the audience to leave quietly as some danger or other has been discovered, only to find those watching remain steadfastly in their seats assuming that it is all part of a modern interpretation of the play. This sense of unease is also present, though in reverse, during audience-participation pieces. Here we are required to join in but the rules of the game are confused and as an audience we feel unsettled if we don't know what's going on. In terms of what was mentioned above we are not sure of the 'contract'. Something is going on but it is out of our hands. If we want to establish a successful drama activity we need, then, to let the children know what is going on and what they are to expect even if what is expected is that we will all join in. If we are clear of the rules then we feel much safer.

    ACTIVITY 3.1

Participation in drama

Think of two drama situations in which you have participated where you felt uncomfortable. What was it that made you feel this way? What did the situations have in common?

Derek recalls with some embarrassment one of his first attempts at drama. Having a student on teaching practice in the class he thought it would be a good idea to show her a drama activity. After play one morning he went into the class (with whom until now he had had a good relationship) with a letter he had written but which he pretended had come from a child called Paul (there being two Pauls in the class). The letter said that they didn't want him as their teacher any more. With an acting bravado worthy of any Oscar he said how betrayed and upset he felt and how he would leave them for five minutes in order that they could sort out what was going on. Derek and the student stood outside the door for five minutes and listened whilst the real-life drama of a class picking on the two hapless boys unfolded. When he re-entered the room and told them it was all just a drama they reacted very aggressively and he found it hard to come to terms with their sense of hurt. There was a drama but it existed only in Derek's mind. For the children it was the reality of one of their group falsely accusing their teacher. They quite rightly felt that the trust that they had placed in Derek had been abused.

When you use drama it is vital that you clearly mark out when you are in the drama and when you are not. As teacher it is your responsibility to indicate the drama time. Some teachers use simple devices such as wearing a hat or the holding of a clipboard to indicate that the drama has begun. When the chosen item has been put down then we all return to being ourselves again. Chris in the previous Unit used a shawl to indicate another role but it also marked the drama time. Terri has tried a number of different strategies but has found the simplest to be that of counting the children into the drama and coming out by saying 'Stop!' As she says, when she used the hat it was never around when she needed it!

The problems caused by poorly-defined drama time are not restricted to inexperienced teachers such as Derek. Terri remembers one occasion working in a special school with a group of children with profound learning difficulties when she went into the classroom dressed as a tramp. The children had to help the tramp who was frightened and hungry. She felt a sense of triumph as the children went to the school canteen to get her a drink and a Mars Bar. Finally she hugged them in turn and left the room. Returning as herself a few minutes later she talked to the children and realized with some unease that the children had in fact not experienced a drama. As far as they were concerned a tramp *had* come into their classroom . They had talked to her and given her a drink and something to eat and now she had gone. What Terri hadn't done was to explain that they were going to make up a story and then to mark out the drama time in an appropriate way.

    ACTIVITY 3.2

Drama time

Compare the lessons of Derek and Terri. What were the similarities? What were the differences? How might you have done each differently to mark the drama time clearly?

BUILDING BELIEF

Having set up the contract with the children Terri goes into the drama. It is important that she moves into the drama slowly, drawing the children into the fiction with her. Before she can get them to look at the real problem that the old lady faces and empathize with her they must put something of themselves into the story. They must feel that they as well as the old lady have something to lose.

Terri starts the drama by reading an imagined extract from a diary. It tells of a woman, Antoinetta, who had come to England from Italy with her husband just after the Second World War and had set up a café. She recounts special memories of the place and how for the people of the local Italian community it became somewhere where they all met together. The children then talk about what the café must have meant to the people who frequented it.

Terri has set up a table with three cups on it and three chairs in the centre of the room. The children stand in a circle around the table and they are invited to take on the role of the people who come to the café. They take it in turns to come up to the table in role, sit down and talk about a memory that they have of the café. These can be happy, sad, or commonplace and they can talk by themselves or to the others at the table. Slowly as the children talk a picture of the café's past emerges. When this has been done the class sits as a group and talks about what has been found out so far and Terri writes the main points down on a large piece of paper. The children then work in small groups to bring to life one of the memories. When they have put together their short improvised presentations Terri sets up the class so that she can walk from group to group as Antoinetta 'going about her job as she moves around the café, and at each table old memories come flooding back'. At the point that she stops the groups enact their presentations.

What Terri is doing here is leading the children into the drama. She is slowly building up the fiction with them so that they feel ownership of the story. As she works she encourages them to commit more of themselves to the work. This has been referred to by Dorothy Heathcote (1984) and others as building commitment or building belief and we go into it in more detail in Unit 5. For the moment let us simply recap on what was said in Unit 1 about the shift from cognitive to affective: it is very difficult for children to go into a drama

Plate 5 The café – children talking in role

situation cold and create some interest and feeling for what is going on. Terri starts off with something that they find engaging, like the diary extract, which simply requires them to listen, then using their ideas she builds up the story. When the climax of the story is arrived at the children will be more involved and more committed to a course of action.

It is important to consider the children's previous experience when beginning drama. Much of the success of a lesson can depend upon what they have done before. Yes, you can launch into a three-hour epic, fully costumed and with the appropriate lighting but for most children in such a case their experience will revolve around the elements of theatre not the dramatic events of the story. With children who haven't done much drama before it might be a good idea to think in terms of an extension activity tacked on to another lesson. It might be, for example, that the children could talk in pairs as if one was a journalist and the other was someone who had been at the Battle of Hastings or had seen the Great Fire of London or whose crops had failed due to the drought. The activity need not take long nor need the chairs and tables be moved. The children are working in a slightly different way, speaking in role on an imaginary topic, yet other things remain the same. Other effective activities that involve simple pair work might include neighbours talking over the events discovered in the reading of the latest chapter of a serial story or colleagues discussing a development plan for a local community. The range of opportunities is only limited by your imagination. But all of these offer safety to the class. Because they feel secure they are more able to participate in the activity. Above all, if the class is new to drama make it clear what is expected of them. Reassure them by telling them what is going to happen and clearly mark out the drama time. Let them know when they're in the story and when they're not. The more comfortable they feel with what is going on around them the more prepared they will be to join in.

PSYCHOLOGICAL DISTANCE

Working in drama often requires an emotional commitment and indeed, as we said earlier, it is at its best when there is one. Children have the potential for getting too involved in what is going on to realize that they are operating in the 'as-if', the make-believe. Think back for a moment to Derek's earlier attempt at drama when he had a student in the class. He went into role as a class teacher and pretended that one of them had sent him a letter. This was far too close to his actual role of teacher. As for the children, they were afforded no psychological protection at all. They were dealing with a reality. We as teachers have a responsibility to protect the children that we work with and when using drama. This is most effectively achieved by constructing distance through the use of role, time and place. Let's take each of these in turn and look at how each can offer protection.

- *Role*
  At its simplest this is best explained by the notion that the further away from your own role the dramatic role is the easier it will be for you to be protected from what goes on in the drama. We need to be sensitive to this. If a class of children are playing the role of a class of children they may well become confused as to whether they are expected to respond in role or as themselves. One of the most effective ways of overcoming this sense of confusion is to put the children in role as 'adults'. The difference is then clear and the opportunities for uncertainty are reduced. If a child has a clear understanding that he or she is a police officer investigating the bullying at school then the child is less likely to take on board what happens to that role.
- *Time*
  In the same way that the selection of a role can afford psychological protection so will setting the drama in a time other than our own. Developing a drama about, say, Ancient Greeks at school will again enable the children to distance themselves from the fiction. The issues and the problems faced may well be very similar to those encountered in their own classroom but by introducing the element of distance the children will be clear that what has been going on is about 'those people there' and not about 'me'. When looking for settings for your dramas, however, don't only think of the past. Think also of setting the fiction in the future.
- *Place*
  This simply refers to setting the dramas in places other than that which we are in. If you begin a drama about a school there is the potential for confusion in the minds of children so make up a name for the fictitious school and set it in a different part of the country. Depending upon the issues that you were dealing with, you could set the story in another part of this country, somewhere else in the world, or even in outer space.

From this we can see that the situation with most potential for confusion would be to set up a drama where the children play themselves in their classroom today. It offers them no protection whatsoever. The best is where they are different people (for example Native Australian Aborigines) in a different time (in the 1850s during the settlement of Australia) in a different place (a bush village).

 ACTIVITY 3.3

Protection in drama (Part A)

Imagine that you want to look at the issue of homelessness through drama. You will need to offer the children protection through distance. Keeping the idea of distancing the work through role, time and place, consider the following:

- Think of *three* different roles that the children could take in order to look at the topic. What would each have to offer? How far is each from the role of the child in the classroom?
- Now see if you can think of three different times when the drama could be set. What has each got to offer?
- Finally where might the drama be set. If you can, think of a range of alternatives. How might these affect the narrative?

Taking all of the elements into consideration which of the possible combinations would offer the greatest protection to the class and which the least?

Returning once more to Terri's drama, she tells the children that they are going to think about what the café means to the people who have used it over the years. She talks about the memories that the café would have. What would it say if it could speak? She tells the children that stuck to the wall above the counter are lots of photographs that have been taken over the past thirty years in the café. Some were of celebrations, some were sad and others were just of groups of friends. When the customers walked by them they knew that they were part of a long line of people who had been here. In small groups the class constructs these 'photos' as still images. Terri moves from group to group encouraging them to develop their ideas and asking questions to help the children make clearer what they are depicting. When ready, these are looked at in turn and discussed by the children. As they move from photograph to photograph a picture of the café and its history evolves.

The children are then arranged by Terri into small groups around the room. She sets the scene. They are in the café. It is a busy afternoon and it is full of locals. When they are at their most hectic an official will arrive from the council with a letter.

She counts down from three to one and the drama begins with the children in role as the customers. When this improvised scene has gone on for a few minutes Terri walks into the drama space. She has taken on the role of the official and stands aloof. She calls for quiet as

Plate 6 Children working on the still image of the café scene

she has an important announcement to make and proceeds to read a letter from the Council Environmental Health Office which contains the key statement, 'Due to the state of the kitchens and the general condition of the café the establishment is to be closed as of this moment.'

Terri then stops the drama and asks the children to think what would have been going through the minds of the people when they heard the news and she goes round the group placing her hand on the children's shoulders 'thought-tapping' them. They speak the thoughts of the customers in turn as she moves around the room building up a sound picture of the café. She then 'replays' the moment and comes in as the official but this time she asks the children to respond as they feel the customers would have responded. Some quietly leave, others become argumentative. Afterwards, when they talked about what had happened the children had clearly picked up on the sense of loss that the people must have felt when the place where they had shared so much was taken away from them.

Out of role Terri talks to them about the family and how they must feel. Through careful use of open and closed questioning she encourages the children to develop the story. They decide that the café was set up by Antoinetta and her husband and that he isn't alive now. He died several years ago when he was still a young man and her three grown up children live locally but do not work in the café. They have got 'better jobs'. Working in small groups they work on improvised scenes showing the dreams and plans that the couple had. When they opened the café it was to be the finest one around. When at first it was successful they would grow into a great chain. When their first child was born she would take over the business when she grew up.

Throughout this part of the drama Terri is not telling the children what to think or what to say. What she is doing is drawing them into the fiction by encouraging them to put their ideas into the story.

Switching roles Terri becomes Antoinetta. The class adopts a group role where it speaks as one person. The class becomes one of her children telling her of the news brought by the council official and talking over what must be done. Finally realizing that it will cost too much to refurbish the class decides that it must close the café for good.

Terri talks to the class as a group about the best way of depicting this and the children choose the closing of the café for the last time. The scene is set with the children sitting in groups round the room and Terri as Antoinetta. As she 'clears' its table each group gets up and says its final goodbyes. Passing through the imaginary door the children begin to line up forming the four walls of the café. When the last customer has left Antoinetta slowly locks the door for the last time and sits in the empty café and listens as the walls speak to her.

We had some fun here....

It was like a second home to me....

Do you remember the parties in the old days? They'd go on till dawn, we'd have breakfast and go straight to work....

A chain of them Antoinetta, we'll have a chain.

Plate 7 The teacher, Antoinetta, leaves the café for the last time

a ACTIVITY 3.4

Protection in drama (Part B)

In the drama work described above there were a number of ways in which protection was offered to the children. One way was through role, another was through clearly marking out the times when the children were in drama, another through rehearsing and talking through with the children what was going to happen at a given moment in the work. Derek believes that it is quite nice for the teachers to have a few surprises up their sleeves so as to keep the tension going.

What do you think Terri would say to Derek to convince him that this might not be the best way of working?

MAKING IT WORK

Terri's drama was successful. It made the children think and it managed to touch them at an emotional level. But drama is notorious for not going according to plan. It is a paradox that it is exactly this sense of uncertainty, the feeling that anything can happen, that makes the process so enabling and exciting for both teachers and pupils alike but it is also the main reason why some teachers shy away from using drama. Whilst it is impossible to cover all eventualities it is useful to conclude this Unit by considering briefly a range of effective devices for making the drama work.

The first and most important point to remember is that the drama is a story and holds the children's attention in much the same way as a serial will. Although special, drama is not a magic carpet that must be ridden until break time, come what may. If you are aware of things not going according to plan, be it the secretary coming in to check on dinner numbers or two children from Year 3 looking for a jumper that they'd lost at playtime, stop the drama, deal with the problem and then restart it as you would if you were reading the class a story. Similarly if the children are not behaving according to the terms of the contract that you've made with them then stop the drama and talk through the problem. It is important to bear in mind that you should not be expected to accept worse behaviour in drama than you would at any other time. If children are going beyond what is reasonable then the normal sanctions for poor behaviour should be applied.

Controlling the child who wants to do everything is also an issue for most teachers and when a child is coming up with a string of good ideas it is often difficult to quieten her or him. The danger is that the individual child will take over the drama. There are a number of actions that can be taken but one of the most effective is to give the child a 'special job' to do. We well remember one child we taught being effectively gagged by being given the role as the 'official note-taker'! Similarly, giving very withdrawn children a special job to do in the drama will mean that they will be drawn into the fiction. With both the very vocal and the very quiet child, working in pairs is a productive strategy. Here the quiet child may well be more prepared to participate whilst the bossy or domineering child will have their sphere of influence limited. And, oh the joy of putting the two bossy children together and letting them get on with it!

KEY POINTS

Children work best when they know what is going on and what is expected of them. So establish a contract and tell them what is expected of them.

Don't forget that you have a responsibility to make the drama interesting for the children.

Children engage more fully in the drama if you as a teacher have drawn them into the story. Help them to build belief and commitment to the work.

It is easier for children to operate in the drama if there is a clear division between the real them and the role they are portraying. Build in protection by establishing distance of role, time and place.

Drama is a shared process. Don't let individuals take over. If you feel that it is happening then give the individual concerned special jobs to do and develop more pair and small group work.

Above all, trust the medium. If the focus is clear and the children feel comfortable and safe then the work should come quite naturally. There is really no one way of working in drama despite all that theoreticians might say. There are a great number of different devices and structures that can be used to enrich the simple unfolding of the story and we shall examine a number of these in the next Unit.

Ways of working: roles and conventions

When Chris started teaching drama she had worked with other practitioners and had begun to build up a range of different ways of working. Terri also has an extensive repertoire of teaching strategies whilst Derek tends to keep to a number of favoured techniques. In this Unit we are going to examine ways of using drama with a class and to begin to develop and explore the effectiveness and appropriateness of these strategies.

When working with children what is central to drama is that they are not simply reproducing reality but are dealing with an art form. As teachers it is not our function to train them in ever more precise mimes nor to create situations so accurate that they are indistinguishable from reality. Both Derek and Terri in their own ways discovered the limitations of this for themselves in the last Unit. The 'ways of working' are the vocabulary that we need to explore the story. As with spoken language the wider the vocabulary the more enriched will be the story that is told.

If you think back to the previous Units in this book one of the common links between all the dramas taught by Terri and Chris is the function of the teacher. In their work they tend to take on the role of one of the characters in the story. This technique is known as teacher-in-role and because of its importance as a way of working we will examine it first.

TEACHER-IN-ROLE

At its simplest teacher-in-role is the teacher participating in the drama and then interacting with the others who are also taking part. The role itself can be a significant one (the leader or the boss) or it can be more discreet. What it creates is a very effective teaching relationship between the teacher and the children. In Unit 2 we discussed at some length the notion of teacher intervention and it is exactly this that makes the strategy so effective. As a teacher using role work not only do you act as a model for the children but you can also guide them to areas of learning that they might very well miss or avoid. As we said in Unit 2 children left to themselves will make up stories but in order to get to the end they will all too frequently take the easy way out. If the story becomes difficult they will invent a 'magic solution'. If the teacher is within the story then much of the shaping and maintaining of focus can be done through the role.

In Unit 2, Chris Johnson was able to get the children to confront the environmental issues inherent in the situation by bringing the role of the mussel farmer to the children. She wouldn't accept the easy way out. She wouldn't let the problem go away. Derek, on the other hand, in his drama on pollution found that the story was moving away from him. The children working within the story ignored the aspect of pollution and set up a fashion show instead. This move away from the issue was because of the lack of opportunities for intervention created by his being outside the fiction. As an onlooker he was powerless to affect the story.

So then, being in role helps the teacher direct the children to explore specific learning areas but once you have decided to take on a role what kind is best? David Booth, a Canadian drama practitioner, is reported to have said in jest, 'I love to do drama because I get to be king' and there are teachers for whom this is true in earnest. Certainly when the teacher and the class are unused to this way of working then such a high-status role can be effective. The nature of the role is not so different from that of the teacher. In this way the relationship between teacher and pupil has not been changed very much. However, if this dominant role is the only one that is ever used by the teacher then the power relationship of the class will always be the same. That is to say, the children will always look towards the teacher-in-role as king, captain, commander, senior researcher or chief cook – in other words, the one with the power, the one who has the information and makes the decisions. By taking on different types of roles the teacher can affect the locus of power in the story. In Terri's drama with the young adults with learning difficulties that we talked about in the last Unit she wanted to give them the feeling of being more able than the tramp that they met. What she had done was to alter the power relationship by changing the status of the character that she had selected in the drama. It was they who knew what to do, not the tramp. The tramp was more frightened than they were and *they* knew how to get to the canteen to buy her the Mars Bar. For one of the few times in their lives they were in a position of authority and control.

Whilst you may never want to go as far as Terri did in her drama what you can do is experiment with other alternatives to the leader role. Dorothy Heathcote (1984) and Morgan and Saxton (1987) have looked at these in some detail and examined the different effects that each might have in the drama. What we now want to do is to consider a few of the most commonly used and useful of these role categories.

Below is a list of broad role types that you can use. Each one will have a different effect on the way that the relationship operates in the drama.

- *High-status role (leader role)*
  This is characterized by the king, the chief technician, the leader. It is the person who has the power in the group and is the person who most often will be at the centre of the story.
- *Opposer role*
  The catalyst in the drama. The one who won't let you do what you want to do. The guard

who won't let you on the train or the doctor who won't let the refugees bring their injured comrade into the hospital.

- *Low status role*
  The tramp in Terri's drama is a good example of this role. Here the group has more knowledge and more power than the role. This shift in relationship is interesting for groups to work with.
- *Second in charge*
  The role in this situation has a degree of power but does not have ultimate power – the final say. You can take things so far but after that (when things get difficult) you must take orders from another.
- *Intermediary*
  Here we have the classic 'job's-worth' role. 'Well I would let you do that but it's more than my job's worth!' A sitting-on-the-fence position, very useful in drama as it enables the teacher to have a range of imaginary characters either outside or at the end of a phone. It also means that you can be involved in the drama but the responsibility for what goes on belongs to someone else.
- *Low status opposer role*
  This is the person who goes against the general trend but has no real influence or overt power. It is the villager who won't let the stranger in or the Viking who thinks it is far too dangerous to go off in the long boats.
- *One of the gang*
  Equal status to the rest of the group, this role is quite difficult as all too often the group forces the teacher into taking on more of a lead so that the role becomes high status.

 ACTIVITY 4.1

Teacher role

Choose one of the dramas mentioned so far in the book. Look at the teacher role that has been used. Which of the categories set out above does it best fit?

Now choose another category of role. What changes in the drama would occur as a result of this alteration?

INTRODUCING THE ROLE

Having selected the type of role that you feel would best fit the drama there are a number of ways of introducing it to the children. The first point to bear in mind is that you don't have to present a full-fledged National Theatre performance of the character. You could start in a very modest way, for example by speaking the thoughts of the character as a monologue while the children watch. They get the sense of the character without as yet engaging with it. This can then be extended by encouraging them to ask questions of the character that enable them to bring it to life for themselves. It becomes a creation as a result of their questions. In the terms that we shall explore in much more detail in the next Unit the children are building belief in the character and are investing in the drama. From this point situations can be established where the children meet the character and the drama can then develop.

Alternatively you may wish to omit the preliminary stages of the construction of the role and start at the point where the children (in role themselves) meet the teacher as a character. Whilst this has more impact and is more 'dramatic' you need to be aware of how comfortable *you* feel in the role that you have selected and how far you are prepared to engage in it.

SIGNING THE ROLE

Irrespective of the way that you introduce the role, whether through a monologue or by interacting with the group, one of the most important points to consider is *signing*. This is explained in much more detail in Unit 6 but simply expressed, it is the way that we give clues about the role we are presenting. Even in everyday life we are constantly giving signals to others about who we are, how we feel and so on. This information is conveyed by:

Plate 8 Teacher in role

- what we wear;
- what we say;
- how we move;
- what we do;
- the tone of our voice;
- the words that we speak.

Actors with many years experience will use all of these signals to convey the role that they are playing. As a teacher it would be difficult to emulate this fully but what we are able to do is utilize some of these skills to improve our in-role characterization.

If we take the notion of costume we can imagine how a theatre designer might wish to create, for example, a tramp – the hat, the old clothes, the matted hair and missing teeth, the bag of possessions and the general look of neglect. As teachers we can't reproduce this effect. We have neither the time nor the resources. But what we can do is to 'sign' a tramp. That is, we are able to choose certain things that give off some signals that indicate 'trampness'. We might for instance choose an old coat to indicate the raggedness of the character. An old hat might be used and perhaps a pair of old woollen gloves. The tramp might also be carrying a bag or a small bundle containing some possessions. He or she might shuffle rather than walk so an old pair of boots might be worn. The voice might be unclear and the tramp may be rather brusque and reluctant to talk.

In Unit 3 you may recall that Terri went into a special school and worked with some young adults and the role she used was that of a tramp. She could not get hold of all the props that we have mentioned above, so she just chose a few which clearly signed 'trampness' to the children she was working with. One might think that the ideal situation when you are working in role would be to have access to the local drama group's costume store. We have found, however, that if you have too many things giving off too many signs then they begin to cancel each other out and instead of the effect becoming stronger the signs get confused and the result is often less effective.

To see how this works let's look at Chris and Derek using the technique of teacher-in-role. In Unit 2 Chris developed a drama about a mussel farmer. Not long after this Derek decided to do a very similar drama where he too was a fisherman. The main difference between the two was that as Derek feels less confident about working in role he used far more in the way of props. This is how the two of them presented their roles.

Chris
- Costume: an old shawl pulled round her shoulders.
- Props: a piece of thick nylon string (from the PE store).
- Voice: softer than her normal voice and slightly hesitant.

Derek
- Costume: stripy t-shirt, scarf round his neck, captain's cap, wellington boots (green), corduroy trousers.
- Props: an old pipe, some netting, a children's telescope.
- Voice: West Country accent, loud, using a lot of seafaring clichés.

ACTIVITY 4.2

Signing in role

Look at the two ways that the role was presented to the children by Chris and Derek.

- Was the signing as clear in both cases?
- What signs do you think were the most effective?
- Which teacher do you think would have been the most effective?
- What do you think the effect on the children would have been?

Derek's role did not work out very well. The children found it hard to believe in his portrayal of a fisherman.

ACTIVITY 4.3

Effective signs

Look at these tools that Derek was using to sign the role of the fisherman:

- stripy t-shirt;
- scarf round his neck;
- captain's cap;
- wellington boots (green);
- corduroy trousers;
- an old pipe;
- some netting taken from a vegetable bag;
- a children's telescope;
- West Country accent;
- loud voice;
- seafaring clichés.

If he was able to keep only three of the items listed above which do you think he should keep so as to provide the strongest set of signs for a fisherman? Why?

For our suggestions see the end of the Unit.

As we saw in Unit 1 the strategy of teacher-in-role is one of the most significant changes that has occurred over the past twenty years in the way that teachers use drama. It is, however, not the only technique available to the teacher and clearly in the dramas described in this book so far we have encountered a number of different ways of working. Dorothy Heathcote (1984) was the first of the theoreticians fully to explore the ranges of strategies available to teachers. She set out a number of examples and ideas that she called conventions which have been much expanded upon by Jonathan Neelands in his book *Structuring Drama Work* (1990). Conventions as ways of working become the process through which the children can explore the story in depth. They take the form of the vocabulary through which the drama is explored and develop naturally out of the story. The problem that we have encountered when working with teachers is that when conventions are presented as a list they tend to be seen as definitive and complete rather than representing our thinking at one moment in time which should be changed and modified to fit the needs of the particular story being worked upon.

Figure 4.1 provides a list of conventions that can be used in drama. It is not definitive nor do the examples provided indicate the only way of using them. Having presented the list we will examine how they can be tailored to fit *your* particular needs within *your* drama.

The main point to remember about conventions is that in drama we are not trying to represent reality. We are dealing with a symbolic form, an art form. What is needed is the matching of conventions to a specific moment within the drama rather than simply using them to fill the next space. Frequently when teachers have been introduced to the notion of convention it has freed them the sense of realism. Not having to make the dramas always like real life has been liberating for the teacher as well as the children. With insufficient understanding, however, teachers can soon slip into the trap of regarding conventions as the drama itself. The result is a series of conventions that the class works through without any regard to the development of a dramatic structure. This will be explored in greater depth in the next Unit, but what is important for us here is the understanding that the story must underlie all the work and that the conventions are the devices that enable us to slow the drama down, to look below the surface and to attain a much deeper and richer understanding of the issues and characters.

    ACTIVITY 4.4

Use of conventions

Look back at the drama in Unit 3. Terri and the class were working on the notion of community and what it meant to be a part of a subculture. Never losing sight of the main thrust of the story, i.e. the closure of the café, they used a great number of conventions to help them explore the issues and recount the events.

- As you go back though the story, list the conventions that were used.
- To what extent did each deepen the understanding of the children?
- To what extent did they move the story along?

1　**Brainstorming**: random ideas of group members are put down on paper without criticism or comment.
2　**Statementing**: individuals from the drama make statements reflecting their thoughts and feelings about a particular character.
3　**Hot-walking**: the group voice thoughts and observations about actions being mimed by a character within the drama.
4　**Pair work**: members of the group working in twos on an improvisation, discussion or other problem-solving activity.
5　**Prepared improvisation**: two or more people performing for the rest of the group after they have all set up the improvisation, worked on a character and decided on the possible outcomes.
6　**Forum theatre**: an improvisation performed by two or more members of a group working on instructions given by the others. The action can be stopped, altered and replayed at will.
7　**Group monologue**: a small group, in role as a single character, talk through the moments of a specific event to build up an emotional and 'factual' picture.
8　**Telephone conversation**: a one- or two-way conversation between characters sharing information or discussing an event.
9　**Role-on-the-wall**: an important role is represented on paper through drawings or words identifying key facts and exploring attitudes, relationships, feelings, etc.
10　**Still image**: using their own bodies, members of the group create an image of an event, idea or theme similar to a waxwork or still photograph.
11　**Hot-seating**: the group working as a whole have the opportunity to 'interview' a character.
12　**Conscience alley**: individuals offer various opinions (as when listening to one's own conscience) as a character tries to make a decision.
13　**Group discussion**: members of the group share ideas on a given point. No written record need be made.
14　**Meeting**: within the drama individuals gather together to discuss plans, make decisions, hear new information or solve problems.
15　**Streams of consciousness**: individuals offer advice but the character is able to return to members of the group for further advice, evidence and guidance.
16　**Giving witness**: personal account given by character(s) about events within the drama.
17　**Alter-ego**: discussion between two characters with the other group members whispering advice as to what to say. This advice can only be 'spoken' by the main characters.
18　**Diary/letter**: written by members of the group either in or out of role as a way of reflecting on and clarifying what has taken place within the drama.
19　**Storyboarding**: breaking down the sequence of events into the main points, then recording them either pictorially or written on paper.
20　**Small group play-making**: devising and improvising a scene/situation/issue which is then enacted.
21　**Living image**: bringing a still image to life with the action being guided by the members of the group.
22　**Image-making**: an abstract group picture rather like a still image but instead of showing a picture of something you show the feelings that inspired it. For example how we might feel about a child's bullying father.
23　**Overheard conversations**: the whole group listen to conversations taking place about matters relating to the drama. By doing this we become aware of different viewpoints.
24　**Promenading**: like overheard conversations. However, the group standing in a circle in twos cross from one side to the other in role discussing a particular event in the drama. We hear only snippets of the conversations which together build up into an overall picture.
25　**Angels and devils**: like streams of consciousness except that one side of the line speaks the thoughts in favour of a particular course of action while the other speaks thoughts against it. The character is able to return to people's thoughts in the line in order to get additional information.
26　**Thought-tracking**: revealing publicly the private thoughts/reactions of role at specific moments in action. Contrasting the outer form with the inner understandings.
27　**Sound tracking**: in the manner of film-makers, i.e. making sounds to fit given pieces of action or in isolation from accompanying action; or as a 'sound picture'.
28　**Re-enactments**: a known event is re-enacted exactly in order to reveal its dynamics and tensions.
29　**Analogy**: working through a parallel situation that mirrors themes and dynamics in the principal situation.
30　**Caption-making**: devising slogans, titles, chapter headings, verbal encapsulations of what is being presented visually. The German playwright Bertolt Brecht used this technique extensively.

Figure 4.1 Drama conventions

Source: Based on N. Kitson and I. Spiby (1989) *Drama Conventions: A Second DIY Guide*, BBC Education

Like most stories in western culture those told in drama need a beginning a middle and an end. The conventions that we use fit into this structure.

1   Some are better at setting the scene.
2   Some build up the interest in the middle of the story.
3   Some are best for exploring the climactic moment.
4   Some are best used during the reflection phases at the end of the drama.

    ACTIVITY 4.5

Structuring conventions

Listed below are four conventions. Match them to the four stages of drama listed above. Which would be the most appropriate to each?

At the end of the Unit you will find the order that we think is the most appropriate.

- *Thought-tracking*: revealing publicly the private thoughts/reactions of role at specific moments in action. Contrasting the outer form with the inner understandings.
- *Small group play-making*: devising and improvising a scene/situation/issue which is then enacted.
- *Hot seating*: the group working as a whole have the opportunity to interview a character.
- *Brainstorming*: random ideas of group members are put down on paper without criticism or comment.

One of the key factors that distinguishes the way that Terri and Derek teach drama is their use of conventions. They are an important tool in developing the story for both of them but what marks them apart is the extent to which the conventions are part of the story rather than a structure that has been simply bolted on to the drama.

Let's look at some of the work that they were both engaged in to explain this difference.

    Terri and her class are doing a drama on the theme of the Victorians and are developing a story about a group of children living in a workhouse near Bristol. They have begun to build up a picture of life in the workhouse, of the conditions and the reasons that people were sent there. To consolidate this Terri wants the children to use the convention of still image to represent the people engaged in activity in the workhouse. She introduces this by telling the children that many years later when the workhouse was being demolished, they found under the floorboards in one of the rooms a sketch book belonging to Betsy, one of the

Plate 9 Hot-seating – the children ask questions of the teacher who is in role

characters in their drama. It contained scenes of the life in the workhouse. She then asks the children to recreate one of the sketches from the old book.

 Derek is working on a very similar theme as it fits into the current Year 5 History scheme of work. First he talks to the children about the Victorians, then about life in a workhouse and asks them to make a still image of something that might have been happening.

The activity in both of the dramas is exactly the same. The children are all participating in the construction of a still image and no doubt they will all do it very proficiently. But there is a significant difference in the way the convention was introduced. For the children in Derek's class the still image is the next 'thing' that they must do and once done they will move on to the next 'thing'. For the children in Terri's class they were building the context of the story. The still images themselves were part of the story – they came from Betsy's sketch book. The activity had been woven into the story and as such the effect was much more powerful and a good deal richer.

This is the key to the effective use of drama conventions. In the final Unit of this book we will go on to examine drama as an art form. That is, we will look at the notion that there is more to drama than a series of activities that could to all intents and purposes be called 'active English'. Not only the structure is important here, but also the way specific sections of the drama are introduced and linked.

Teachers in our experience, when introduced to conventions, often develop what has been referred to as the 'Chinese Restaurant' notion of drama teaching. Here they will pick from the list of conventions, either selecting at random or choosing the old favourites with a few new ones to sustain the children's interest – 'A Number 42 followed by a 12, and then a 35.' This, clearly, is not the most effective way of teaching. The resulting work lacks any real sense of dramatic development and aesthetic shape. What is important is to let the convention meet the needs of the drama rather than fitting the drama around the conventions that you have chosen. Think back to the two uses of the same drama convention by Derek and Terri described above. The conventions must be given some context that relates to the drama. As a result they will take on a much greater significance, they will be seen much more as part of the structure and they will enrich the learning experience of the children.

The same convention can be presented in a wide number of ways if the context is frequently changed and the children will perceive it as a) new and different and b) a true development of the drama. Let's now look at how this might work in practice by taking the convention of conscience alley.

> *Conscience alley*: individuals offer various opinions (as when listening to one's own conscience) as a character tries to make a decision.

This is most often arranged with the children standing in two parallel lines facing inwards, about six feet apart. In order to elicit the 'thoughts', someone (and most often that is the teacher) walks down the line and when she or he stands in front of each member of the group they speak their 'thoughts'. Now don't misunderstand us, there is nothing wrong with this as a way of working but if it is repeated too many times then the children begin to see it as an activity rather than a part of the drama. With very little effort, however, it can be improved upon. Let's say that the class are working on Terri's drama about the Victorians. In it she has set up the situation where there are three children, Jed, Alice and Betsy, who run away from a workhouse. She wants to use the convention conscience alley to encourage her class to think about how the three children might have felt as they made up their minds as to whether or not they should run away.

 Procedure A

She set up the two lines telling the children that the workhouse where the children were living was old and forbidding. It was full of dark and gloomy corridors. The very walls of the workhouse had seen so much over the years that at times people almost felt that they could speak. As the children crept down the corridor to escape from their plight the walls spoke to the children with the insight of all those hundreds of children that had lived there. What did the walls advise them as they fled?

Procedure B

The children in the workhouse were lining up to collect their meagre evening meal. They had as usual formed into two lines. News had got round that the three children were going to run away. As Jed, Alice and Betsy walked back down the line having collected their food, what advice did the other children whisper to them?

Procedure C

Jed, Alice and Betsy are making their way towards the wall which once they are over, will signify freedom. The line of children represent their thoughts. As they approach the wall their minds are filled with a mass of contradictory advice. Some of it tells them to go and some says stay. By the time they get to the end of the line they will have listened to all the advice and will have to decide on the basis of the advice whether they should climb the wall or return to the workhouse. What do their 'consciences' tell them to do?

You can see that these three procedures are clearly based on the same convention but the way that each has been presented alters the way that it is seen by the class. Each of them has a slightly different feeling and creates a different atmosphere. The teacher has flexibility of choice to select the most appropriate for the moment in the drama. It may be that she wants the sense of foreboding in Procedure A, the sense of secrecy of Procedure B, or the turmoil of thought created by Procedure C.

In the next Unit we will develop the sense of building up the drama and explore further the whole notion of structuring, but before we leave the discussion of conventions try this final activity.

 ACTIVITY 4.6

Conventions in context

Look at this description of the convention of statementing.

> *Statementing*: individuals from the drama make statements reflecting their thoughts and feelings about a particular character.

Think back to the Bullying drama in the Introduction. The convention of statementing is used to build up a picture of Jason, the victim. Imagine that you go on to create a similar picture of Andrew, the bully, again using statementing. As with the example above (Terri's lesson on the workhouse) think of three different contexts around which the convention can be constructed.

When you have done this consider the atmosphere and feelings that could be created. Which would you select as being the most interesting and engaging for your class?

 ANSWERS AND SUGGESTIONS

Activity 4.3 Effective signs

From the selection of forms of signing available we would have chosen the following three:

Pipe
Captain's cap
Seafaring clichés (though we would try to use the language forms rather than
the clichés)

Activity 4.5 Structuring conventions

There are a number of ways that these conventions can be combined but we feel
that this would be the most immediate.

1   Some are better at setting the scene.
    Brainstorming: random ideas of group members are put down on paper
    without criticism or comment.
2   Some build up the interest in the middle of the story.
    Hot-seating: the group working as a whole have the opportunity to
    interview a character.
3   Some are best for exploring the climactic moment.
    Small group play-making: devising and improvising a scene/situation/issue
    which is then enacted.
4   Some are best used during the reflection phases at the end of the drama.
    Thought-tracking: revealing publicly the private thoughts/reactions of role
    at specific moments in action. Contrasting the outer form with the inner
    understandings.

Aspects of theatre in drama teaching

Chris Johnson is teaching a drama lesson about crime. Like many of us she is concerned about the violence on television and films and the way that the children seem to be desensitized by it. She wants therefore to try to bring her class to a point where they look at the consequences of violent crime, to see it as the sordid business it is, rather than the glamorous media portrayal.

We want to use this lesson as a starting point for examining the way successful drama lessons are structured in practical terms. Therefore rather than a discursive description of the lesson, we will outline the way that one stage develops into another, with just enough information to keep you informed about what is happening.

CRIMINALS

1   Chris leads a class discussion about criminals. What do really big criminals do? What sort of crimes? We are going to look at criminals who are successful – and who commit major, violent crimes.
2   Work in twos. Each of them is going to be a criminal. They discuss what sort of crimes they do. No petty criminals are permitted – shoplifters and the like. They've got to be big and they've got to be successful.
3   Chris tells the class that they are going to set up a scene where big-time criminals agree to be interviewed on television. What sort of safeguards would they, as criminals need? A number of suggestions given: anonymity, a secret location for the interview, bodyguard protection, etc.
4   They set up the studio. Decide where they will sit, where interviewer will sit, where the (non-existent) cameras will be.
5   With the class standing round the edge of the classroom, Chris narrates their arrival at the studio. She uses deliberately heightened language and evocative, descriptive words.

('The studio is on an old disused airfield. Through the mist in the early morning, one by one, large, black limousines arrive, etc.') As she narrates, when each person feels ready, they walk onto the 'set' and sit down.

6   In role as the presenter, Chris thanks them for coming, assures them of safeguards, says she is waiting for the green light from the television director and then begins the programme. She introduces them using first names only and then asks questions. What sort of crimes, what enjoyment do they get, what are the advantages, what are the disadvantages, would they consider going straight – and so on? After a while she wraps up the programme, thanks them for coming, says goodbye.

At this point Chris finishes the lesson. It has taken nearly an hour. The interviews went on longer than she had thought they would but the kids were interested and involved; she wanted to give as many people as possible the chance to speak. She picks up the drama again during the next lesson.

7   After a brief recap she tells them she wants to concentrate on one criminal who will no longer be the child's who created it but will 'belong' to everyone. Everyone will contribute to it. They choose a drug baron who not only organizes the growing and sale of drugs but also murders indiscriminately anyone who gets in his way. They decide to call him 'Mr D'.

8   Chris asks the children to be people who work for Mr D. None of them has actually been hurt by him but they know him. They've seen how he works and how ruthless he can be – but also how good he can be to those who please him. They are all frightened of him. One of the main rules he insists on is that no one talks to anyone else. Despite this rule, she asks the class in groups to make up a whispered conversation about him, swapping stories, looking over their shoulders all the while. When they have practised, the rest of the class 'overhears' this conversation group by group. She joins in each talking group with the sole purpose of asking the children questions, deepening their responses.

9   Chris now turns her attention to the victims of Mr D. In rather larger groups (7 or 8) she asks them to construct a montage which consists of a series of snippets of dialogue and action only a few seconds in length and which depicts the effect of Mr D's actions on a person and that person's family over a series of weeks, months or even years.

10 The class views the montages and talks about what they are saying. A class discussion and reflection upon the way that Mr D's actions have consequences follows.

The lesson ends here. It has taken about 50 minutes.

11 Chris performs a monologue as Mr D, boasting about his success, pouring scorn on the 'losers' from whom he makes his money. At the same time she conveys some sense of guilt by, for example, over-emphasizing that he doesn't care about the way innocent people are affected by his drugs. He thinks about the way his mother brought him up but then pushes that aside. She didn't understand the ways of the world.

12 The class in groups of four performs a group monologue from a family member of one of the victims. Sitting facing one another, one person in the monologue starts to talk. When he or she runs out of ideas, someone else picks up the threads, and so

on. Chris asks them to tell the *story* of one of the victims from the point of view of the family.

13   Chris now says she would like Mr D to have to face up to these things he has done. It would be no good having a realistic situation because he wouldn't listen. She tells them that Shakespeare wrote a play about a wicked king, *Richard III*. (She leaves aside questions of Shakespeare's bias in the play for another time.) In it he writes a scene where just before a great battle, the ghosts of the people he has murdered appear to him. She reads an annotated version of Act V, Scene iii (see Appendix III). They talk about how Shakespeare creates a sense of nightmare and pressure on the King by using repeated phrases, characters speaking together and so on. They discuss how they might enact the scene with Mr D, using Shakespeare's ideas. Their aim is to make Mr D see how wicked and wrong he has been. They decide that they should *show* him the evil that he has done as well as *tell* him. In groups of three they prepare what they are going to say to him. Chris says she'll take the role of Mr D so that they have someone to play to. They arrange where they want her to be and where each group should be. They decide to start and end each mini-scene with the words 'Despair and die' which then give the cue for the next group to start and so on.

14   They have a run-through and Chris makes it really hard for them. She is not easily persuaded to give up her bad ways!

15   They discuss together how each group can improve its persuasive powers and then run the scene again. Chris leaves the scene at the end with everyone uncertain as to whether she has been converted or not.

16   She calls a meeting, in role as Mr D, of all the people who work for him and tells them about the dream – he has decided to give up his drug empire and he wants their advice as to what to do. A lively debate ensues as to whether he should turn himself over to the police, give his money to the poor and so on.

17   Chris asks each person to write his or her own ending to the play.

We can see that this outline has a fairly straightforward structure and this will provide us with a useful starting point to analyse drama structures in general. For ease of identification later we will call it the **basic method**. The first thing you will notice, of course, is that Chris does not operate a model based on a replication of everyday life – she uses a number of conventions which, as we have explained in the previous Units, enable her to break free from the narrative (this happens and then this and then this) to investigate matters in depth. On the other hand the story-line is important because that is what provides the 'hook' which will keep the children's interest. They will want to stay with the drama in order to find out what happens. Chris meanwhile has other ideas as well. She wants them, as we said at the beginning, to gain some appreciation that crime and violence have consequences for the victims and others – and to appreciate it at an *affective* level. Many of the class would be able to tell you before the drama started that crimes involve victims and isn't it awful. But they would be doing so from a cognitive perspective; the full implications would not be there.

In his book *Drama and Education* Brian Watkins (1981) provides a neat way of starting a drama which we have found extremely useful over the years. He says that you begin with an **enquiry** into the subject followed by a **definition** of the context:

Plate 10 Teacher and children discuss how to improve and re-run the scene

Who is the drama about?
When is it taking place?
Where is it set?
What (broadly speaking) is happening?

We can see that Chris follows this pattern. Section 1, where she discusses criminals and their crimes constitutes the enquiry. The awareness of the class is raised about the subject, people share ideas and so on. She could have done this in other ways such as giving out newspapers and asking the children to find the crime reports. More simply she could have read out a series of crime headlines – or she could have displayed cut-out pictures from newspapers and magazines with 'crime labels' attached to them. The point of the exercise though, is that ideas are brought forward to avoid stereotypes or everyone just following the obvious. In Sections 2 and 3 she provides the definition. The drama is about particular, successful big-time criminals whom the children choose for themselves. It is taking place in the present time (not in the future or some historical past). It is set in a makeshift television studio in a secret location on a deserted airfield and broadly what is happening is that the criminals have agreed to be interviewed for a television programme. The teacher is going to take the role of the interviewer and presenter of the programme.

We want to stress just how important it is to get this right. We have often seen drama lessons fail at the first post because the enquiry and definition are too vague – 'We're going to do a drama where some criminals talk about themselves' is not precise enough either for the children or for the teacher. If you know before you start exactly what you are going to say in the first few minutes and exactly what you expect the children to do, you will have provided a focus that lets everyone know where they are or – to repeat Dorothy Heathcote's phrase – you 'grab their attention and let them know what's up'!

ACTIVITY 5.1

Enquiry and definition (Part A)

Go back to the dramas already outlined in this book and imagine you are going to teach them. Decide precisely how you would establish the who, when, where and what, listed above. Don't just think in general terms. Say out loud (or if necessary write down) exactly what you are going to say to the class and what you are going to ask them to do to start with.

Through this Unit we're going to ask you gradually to plan and structure a drama for yourselves from scratch. Because we will keep returning to it, it might be a good idea to write down your plan on a separate sheet of paper. You'll then quickly be able to see how far you have got each time you reach the Activity which asks you to plan the next section. You have decided, for whatever reason, that you want your class to investigate 'travellers' and consider the prejudice they often experience. We will provide a focus for you to begin by the title: *A Traveller called Danny*

ACTIVITY 5.2

Enquiry and definition (Part B)

A Traveller called Danny

Look first at the Enquiry. What sort of enquiry do you need to make? Do you need to do some research – find out more about travellers – before the drama? And then when you begin, how are you going to introduce it? How are you going to raise the class's level of awareness of 'travellers'? Pictures? A diary of a traveller? A newspaper account? A monologue with you in role as, say an old traveller?

Next decide on the Definition. 'What's up?' Who is Danny – a boy or man? What has happened to him? Is he in trouble of some kind? Accused of theft? Run away? If he's a boy, is he violent to other children in his class? Who are you all going to be? Teachers at his school? Police? Fellow travellers? What situation are you going to create, where? Decide precisely what you are going to say.

TEACHING TIP

If you set the class in role as children it's a good idea to make them older than their actual age. It prevents them going round on their knees with their thumbs in their mouths – a common characterization of children by children!

Returning to the Criminals drama, if we look at Sections 4–8, we will see that they are all to do with establishing the main protagonist in the drama. Nothing much actually *happens* in terms of narrative. No major crime is perpetrated, no police investigation is set in motion. We are finding out about big-time criminals, followed by Mr D in particular and incidentally those who work for him. You might ask – why not go straight to Mr D? After all he's who the drama is really about. Why spend a quite considerable time interviewing big-time criminals in general?

This brings us to another crucial point in planning and structuring which we referred to briefly in Unit 4. It is often called 'building belief' but we prefer to call it 'building commitment'. After having supplied the 'hook' we talked about earlier to catch the children's attention (i.e. the chance to be big-time criminals) we then have to do things that will so engage their interest that they become *involved*. The people in the drama and the subject must actually matter.

TEACHING TIP

In their handbook *Writing Scripts for Television, Radio and Film* (1981) Willis and D'Arienzo provide a pithy quotation which is every bit as true for the drama teacher as it is for the playwright: 'Two things can lick a play. One is that the audience doesn't believe it, and the other is that they don't care.'

The first time Derek Howes tried a drama lesson, he decided it would be a good idea to tackle an environmental issue. He would do a drama about a motorway being built through a village. There would be lots of tension, the kids could organize protest meetings, there could be a Public Enquiry where debate would be lively and the issues thrashed out. Brilliant. This is what drama should be about.

He told the class that they were going to do some drama and he would be taking part. They made a contract about rules and so on. So far so good. Going on to tell them that they were to be members of a village, he asked them to think of who they were and what jobs they did, etc. He then called a meeting and came into it as a council official whose message was that a motorway was planned that would involve the demolishing of the village. They would be moved to the next village a couple of miles away where new houses with all mod cons were being specially built. The kids accepted this without demur. Some were even enthusiastic – which, of course, was the very opposite reaction to what Derek expected.

Collapse of stout party and much asking of questions in the staffroom – 'What did I do wrong?'

What he did wrong was to fail to 'build commitment'. The children had no involvement in the village, no engagement with it. It didn't matter to them whether it was demolished or not. In the Criminals drama, the fact that they are all criminals appearing on television gives them a chance to fantasize but also gives them a sense of importance. They are asked serious questions about what it's like to be a criminal, and as each answer is forthcoming and treated seriously by the teacher-in-role so the engagement with the drama grows. Chris helped it along by creating imaginative settings through language and by the use of dramatic tension (which we will deal with in more detail later). The key to successful building of commitment is to move slowly (but not too slowly so that the children become bored) without taking the story on too much and by making the children *struggle* with something. In this case it was that they were having to create for public consumption ideas on what it is like to be a successful villain. In another drama it could involve physical actions like piecing together an old letter which has been torn up and partly burned or even looking at a map and deciding the best route to take for an expedition into the jungle. In all cases, the children are encouraged to *build upon* a fiction of their own creating.

TEACHING TIP

Don't ask the children to 'be' a character (be a criminal, be a pirate). Ask them to be a character *doing* something (appearing on television, piecing together a map, deciding which route to take).

 ACTIVITY 5.3

Building commitment (Part A)

Suggest some ways in which Derek might have built up commitment to the village community in the Motorway drama before introducing his council official to inform them of the proposed plans.

Some of our suggestions can be found in the 'Answers and Suggestions' section at the end of the Unit.

ACTIVITY 5.4

Building commitment (Part B)

Select one of the dramas outlined earlier in the book. Imagine that you are going to teach it to your class. First identify how the outline indicates that commitment is built. Then formulate for yourself how exactly you would set this up, what words you would use and so on. Go through it, imagining your class in front of you and speaking out loud. Try to foresee any problems that might occur in your particular situation and deal with them before they arise.

 ACTIVITY 5.5

Building commitment (Part C)

A Traveller called Danny

Look back at Activity 5.2. Remind yourself of what you have decided to do to start the 'traveller' drama. From the enquiry and the definition, now decide how you are going to build commitment to this drama. As in the previous activities, think of your class and your situation. Plan precisely how you are going to set up the activities you choose. What are you going to say? Practise it speaking aloud.

Returning once more to our drama on criminals, after the building commitment sections we move on to the main part of the drama which runs from Sections 9–15. If you look back at the drama you'll notice that once again there isn't a great deal of action in terms of gun battles, chases, fights and arrests – the kind of things children are used to if they have a regular diet of television cartoons and American cop series. And it is the greatest mistake to try to give them a version of that in classroom drama. If you do you are likely to have the children running up the walls, receive complaints from next door and bring yourself to an early grave; quite apart from the fact that educationally you'll be doing them few favours.

The high point of all good drama is that there is a disturbance of the status quo, after which things will never be the same again. The deeper and more profound that disturbance is, the deeper and more profound will be the affective response which in turn will lead to a deep and profound (cognitive) reflection. Therefore Chris, when planning the drama, decided that a nightmare, where Mr D is confronted by the shades of his victims, should be her main or climactic scene. If it was done properly then the status quo would be changed and Mr D would never be the same again.

ACTIVITY 5.6

Moving too quickly

We want you to consider the all important matter of moving slowly in drama, how you dilute the power if you rush at the climactic scene.

Go back in the drama to Section 8, the overheard conversation with Mr D's associates and then move straight to Section 14 where Mr D's nightmare is enacted. Why precisely would this be weak dramatically?

You'll find some of our reasons at the end of the Unit.

It will be useful now to look at the climax in more detail and see how exactly Chris makes it work and what the implications are. The first point that probably strikes you when reading it in the lesson outline is that after building commitment and then moving slowly towards the main scene, when finally reaching it Chris still does not allow the pace to speed up. She introduces the extract from *Richard III*, they talk about it, run through their nightmare scene, talk about that and then enact it one more time. We can see by this that she actually understands the drama process well and since the first time we met her teaching the Bullying drama she has come a long way. A less experienced teacher would have been tempted to keep the nightmare scene up her sleeve until the last moment and then spring it on the children on the assumption that because it is highly dramatic, they would become engrossed in it in the way that an audience would react to a similar scene in the theatre or on film. Once the element of surprise has gone the argument goes, then the scene becomes less intense, less appealing. This line of reasoning shows a fundamental misunderstanding of the process for *participants* rather than *audience*. If the children are an audience watching the teacher's drama, then a dramatic surprise is going to be very thrilling, and repeating it may lessen its effect. If they are participants in a drama of their own and the teacher's devising, then repeating in order to 'get things better' will actually increase its effect. (There is a sense in which children participating in a drama are also members of their own audience. We have defined the categories separately to simplify the point we wish to make.) We only have to look at the way children repeat enjoyable episodes in their own personal play to appreciate the truth of this remark.

There are occasions, of course, when it is valid to produce a surprise if it contributes genuinely to the dramatic action, but what it tends to do is prevent the children having control of the dramatic and theatrical form. In Chris's case she deliberately introduced the Shakespeare extract in order that they would work with the form of the drama as well as the content. By looking at how Shakespeare created his scene (use of repetition, heightened language and so on) they could shape theirs in a more informed way. The opportunity to try it out once before discussing amendments meant that they were able to deal with the drama as an art form, arising out of their affective experience. If they went on actually to perform the Shakespeare text, they would bring to it more understanding and a more genuine theatrical feeling than if they had simply taken the text first and tried to work towards a feeling. This illustrates cogently the point made in Unit 1 about moving from the affective to the cognitive rather than vice versa.

 ACTIVITY 5.7

The climax (Part A)

Look at the description of dramas elsewhere in the book and locate in each what you think is the climactic scene.

How is this scene reached? Would it affect the drama if one of the intervening scenes were removed – or if another were added?

In what way are the children aware of the *form* of the drama? If they are not, can you think of ways in which they might be if you were to teach that lesson.

TEACHING TIP

One of the most difficult things for a playwright (or a drama teacher) to judge is whether they are going too fast or too slow in the build-up of the drama. Go too fast and the climax is spoiled, go too slow and the audience (or children) get bored.

Drama teachers have the advantage over playwrights because they are making up the drama with the audience/participants there at the time. Watch for signs that the children are still interested and go as slowly as you can. Plan more scenes than you need and be prepared to cut some out if necessary.

 ACTIVITY 5.8

The climax (Part B)

A Traveller called Danny

Remind yourself how far you've got with your Traveller drama. Decide what your climactic scene is going to be. Remember it is something where the status quo is changed. How are you going to build up to it? Are there some scenes that you could jettison if necessary? Which are the essential scenes that must be kept in at all costs?

TEACHING TIP

An aspiring playwright friend of ours was lucky enough to have his play accepted by a large repertory theatre with a well-respected professional director. Working through the play with this director he was told that he had to get rid of any scene which didn't 'move the action along'. For our purposes this means that every scene we do must tell us something more than we know already.

The final part of the drama is a resolution of the action. Having presented a scene in which the status quo is changed we have a compulsion to find out 'what happened'. It is here once again that Chris shows her growing expertise as a drama teacher. What everyone wants is for Mr D to be converted and see the light, rather like Ebenezer Scrooge in *A Christmas Carol*. But it takes an expert like Dickens to make it work like that. (You will remember that Scrooge goes through a *series* of traumatic experiences including facing his own death before he is in a position to change his ways.) For Mr D just to say he's sorry, with promises to be good in future, would be a let-down, pleasing on a surface level maybe, but ultimately unsatisfactory. Hence Chris's decision to make the children work at the drama to the bitter end. Through the meeting, she puts before the class the implications of a change of heart and prevents an easy solution, just as would any playwright worth their salt. And at the conclusion of the drama, each child has to make their own decision, writing their own ending.

ACTIVITY 5.9

The resolution (Part A)

Look back at the dramas outlined in the book and for each one, view the resolution. Is there an easy conclusion? Do the children really have to struggle to come up with an answer to the problem set? If they don't, how would you alter the drama to achieve this end?

ACTIVITY 5.10

The resolution (Part B)

A Traveller called Danny

Plan the final part of your Traveller drama remembering what we have said about not providing an easy solution.

This then is the basic outline of a structure that is commonly used in drama-in-education and which if you remember we have termed the **basic method**. It follows a familiar pattern and one that we can find in the vast majority of stories and dramas (on television and film for example) with which children will be familiar. It is sometimes known as the Aristotelian structure, although confusingly Aristotle did not invent it. The pattern, reduced to its barest minimum is as follows:

1   *Exposition*
    The main characters of the drama together with the basic situation are revealed. The problem with which the drama will be concerned is outlined.
2   *Rising action*
    The events of the drama occur, each one building in intensity. The characters in the drama struggle with the problem and experience a series of set-backs, not so difficult as to make them give up but not so easy that they can be overcome without exertion.
3   *Climax or crisis*
    The high point of the drama where the struggle is at its most intense. The status quo is changed.
4   *Resolution or denouement*
    The drama is rounded off, the problem is resolved, the outcome ascertained and the subsequent fate of the characters decided.

So common and widespread is this structure, so embedded in our consciousness, that a case could be made for saying that we are programmed to accept it. This is most noticeable when in a drama one ingredient is faulty or missing. For example, as spectators of drama we are 'programmed' to expect that there will be a winding-down period after the climax which works psychologically to help us adjust to the change of status quo. In the last of the *Black Adder* series on television, *Black Adder Goes Forth*, the writers decided in the final episode to end on the climax and dispense with any resolution. This they did deliberately for dramatic effect. So, as these comic First World War soldiers in the trenches, whom we had grown to love and laugh at, went over the top in the final seconds of the programme, the picture froze and the credits rolled and we, stunned, realised they had all just been killed. The effect was profoundly disturbing, as letters in subsequent issues of the *Radio Times* verified.

All this points to the fact that as drama teachers we would be foolhardy if we did not follow this common pattern. It does not mean, however, that the structure of all drama lessons has to be identical; there are numerous variations and we will outline the main ones.

The Aristotelian structure is most noticeable perhaps in the much-vilified 'well-made play'. Here the convention throughout is one of realism; the actors try to give the impression that what they are enacting is a 'slice of life' although of course it is highly artificial in the way it is arranged. The play consists of a series of 'realistic' scenes where the problem is encountered, grappled with and finally resolved. It is the one with which children will be most familiar but because everything has to be done as if it was real, it is the most difficult in trying to create a successful drama. For example, the exposition normally consists of people in the drama telling one another what they already know, for the benefit of the audience and it requires great skill on the part of a playwright not to make it sound contrived and silly.

The most common design of the well-made play, and one brought to near-perfection by the Norwegian dramatist Henrik Ibsen, is to set the play just before the moment when the crisis is about to erupt. We learn about the characters and the situation that led up to the crisis in retrospect as the climactic moment gets nearer and nearer. It works well realistically because people can tell one another what has happened in the past without resorting to non-realistic conventions. In fact, Ibsen often introduces a character who has returned after many years away and is therefore in a position to be told what he or she is not likely to know. This technique works well dramatically because, with the impending climax, we are constantly in a state of tension and expectancy. For ease of identification we will call this the **Ibsen method**.

Judith Ackroyd (1994) describes her school drama *Susie and the Snow* which uses such a structure but in drama-in-education terms. The teacher begins by reading an extract from Susie's diary which confesses that she is frightened of going out in the snow and hints at something terrible that happened in the past which will account for this. The children interview Susie (teacher-in-role) and eventually the terrible event is revealed. Despite warnings from parents and friends, Susie went skating on the river, fell through the ice and only narrowly escaped being drowned. The children are then given the task of resolving her situation and tackling her fear. Where Ackroyd differs from Ibsen is that she uses non-realistic conventions and an overt use of theatricality to make the drama work. (We will be referring to the latter in the next Unit.)

 ACTIVITY 5.11

The Ibsen method

Look at the Criminal drama at the beginning of the Unit. See if you can re-arrange the structure so that it conforms to Ibsen's method described above, but using non-realistic drama-in-education conventions.

(You would need to start somewhere near the point of Mr D's nightmare. How are you going to introduce him? Remember you still have to 'hook' the children, build commitment and work towards the climax.)

Throughout this book we have emphasized the use of non-realistic drama conventions which are used in order that we might slow down and deepen the work we do. And although non-realism is commonplace in the theatre it is not the dominant style that children are likely to be used to in their encounters with drama on television. One thing they *will* find easy to accept, however, and which is very different from the Ibsen style of realistic drama, is what we have termed the **montage** effect. Rather than unfolding a single plot in a logical, progressive fashion, dramatists these days, influenced no doubt by the television medium, write a series of small scenes which may on the surface seem unrelated but which link together overall to a theme or line of development. Contemporary audiences have been trained to hold many pieces of a seemingly unrelated jigsaw in their minds and are able to make sense of them by the time the drama is finished. Indeed, a television series like *Casualty* often has pieces of up to four jigsaws being placed before the viewer in any one episode. Children too have this rather sophisticated facility and we should not underestimate their ability to make sense of a number of dramatic themes. Having made that point, we can now offer a further structure which we will identify as the **montage/theme method**.

Caryl Churchill in her play *Vinegar Tom* (1985) uses such a method to explore the theme of witchcraft. Talking about the research for the play she says:

> I discovered for the first time the extent of Christian teaching against women and saw the connections between medieval attitudes to witches and continuing attitudes to women in general. The women accused of witchcraft were often those on the edges of society, old, poor, single, sexually unconventional; the old herbal tradition of the cunning woman was suppressed by the rising professionalism of the male doctor.

In the play a number of women in a village, fitting variously into the categories described above, are accused of witchcraft through the ignorance and superstition of their neighbours. They are all eventually hanged. If we wanted to use this theme for a drama lesson in school we might also use the montage/theme method. The various women could be established together with the reasons why they might be accused of witchcraft, moving then through building commitment to the climactic scene where the women are 'tested' for witchcraft (a test, of course, which does not permit innocence). Their hanging comes as a matter of course so the resolution would be a consideration of how and why such accusations occurred. And perhaps, what are the parallels in contemporary society.

One final version of our method of structuring concerns how we view the dramatic concept of 'action'. As we hinted earlier in the anecdote about our aspiring playwright friend, action is anything that moves the drama along, even though in the popular mind it consists of car chases, gun fights and the like. One form of action in the sense we mean it can be the development of a character throughout the drama. The character starts off as one person but as the drama evolves gradually changes so that by the end we could almost say he or she is another person. We've identified this approach as the **character/action method**. There is a sense in which we are in the realms of high drama here: characters such as Shakespeare's King Lear or Chekhov's Nina Mihailovna come to mind. But in spite of such an august heritage, it is possible to structure a drama in school in this way and we describe such a drama in detail (*The Roman Soldier*) at the beginning of the next Unit. Before the final activity we think it would be a good idea to turn to Unit 6 and read through this drama.

KEY POINTS

Basic method: starts with exposition followed by rising action which leads to a climax and ends with the *denouement*.

Ibsen method: begins near the moment of climax, and the events that led up to that point are gradually revealed. The climax then occurs, followed by the *denouement*.

Montage/theme method: consists of a number of scenes not necessarily logically connected as a narrative but revolving round a theme. A high point is reached in the drama where the explorations of the theme come to fruition.

Character/action method: deals with the journey (spiritual, moral, physical or otherwise) of a particular character so that by the end they have changed irrevocably from what they were.

 ACTIVITY 5.12

Reviewing the structures

Remind yourself once again of how the different methods of structuring a drama work in practice. Think of something you are teaching at the moment (or will be in the near future) that would be appropriate for drama and decide which method would suit the material. Once you have decided, rough out what the main elements of the drama would be.

Having now come to an understanding of how dramas work in practice and how you can use this knowledge to plan and structure your own in a school situation, we turn to the final Unit which deals with the all-important matter of understanding theatre form and how to apply it when you actually come to do the drama.

ANSWERS AND SUGGESTIONS

Activity 5.3 Building commitment (Part A)

Some suggestions:

Family groups
Mimes of everyday occupations
Photographs of past events: winning the cricket match
Family history
Coming home from the war
Local heroes

Activity 5.6 Moving too quickly (i.e. from Sections 8–14)

Some of our reasons are as follows:

- We have not had chance to identify with the victims, understand their plight, *empathize* with them.
- We don't have time to get to know Mr D further. We do this through what the victims say. We need to have our indignation raised against him and what he has done.
- We don't have the benefit of learning what a master dramatist (Shakespeare) has done in a similar dramatic situation. We do not have the chance to learn from his rich language and the resonances he is able to create in the scene.
- Going straight into Section 15 is likely to produce something quite theatrically weak from the children. *Richard III* plus reflection on theatre form plus the chance to practice really does build up the power in dramatic terms.
- It lacks tension – there is no build-up. The 'surprise' of the nightmare is sprung too quickly.

Planning and structuring

As part of Key Stage 2 History, Terri Routhwaite's class have been learning about the Romans in Britain and Terri feels that they are now in a position to put what they have learned to use in a drama. You will remember from the Introduction that Terri is a very experienced teacher of drama and not only has her class had the benefit of this experience throughout their year with her but a strong tradition of drama exists in the school. The children therefore no longer rely on her to give them guidance for every move. While she has certain things that she wants them to tackle (and they know and appreciate this), they have an understanding of theatre form and frequently surprise her by the creative ideas they come up with in response to the tasks she sets.

The outline of the lesson will serve a double purpose: a) to illustrate how the elements of theatre can be used in a classroom drama and b) to show, as we mentioned in the last Unit, how action in drama can be through the development of character.

THE ROMAN SOLDIER

1   Terri gathers the class together and tells them she wants to do a drama with them about a Roman soldier called Flavius. He's part of the invading force to Britain and he's involved in a battle. During this conflict he finds himself fighting with a British prince in hand-to-hand combat and he wins. She asks them in twos to devise a fight in slow motion which will look as realistic as possible. But she reminds them (as she has done many times before) that when actors fight, enormous care is taken to see that they don't actually get hurt. Their skill is making it seem real when it isn't. She asks them to devise the fight in a series of ten moves, ending with Flavius about to kill the Prince (he doesn't do it!). They have time to practise and then as they perform she accompanies them with a brief narration. The ending of this narration is important, conveying the information that as Flavius lifts his sword to plunge it into his opponent's body, their eyes meet and

he hesitates. The Prince mumbles some words that the Roman can't quite hear and then something makes Flavius raise his head. What he sees coming towards him makes his blood freeze …

2   The class naturally wants to know what happened and Terri promises them that they will come back to the fight again but they have a lot of work to do on how Flavius got to be where he was. But before even that, she says, she wants to know what *qualities* a Roman soldier had to possess. She gets some ideas very quickly – after all the children have been working on this very thing. If they had been inexperienced she probably would have then done a role-on-the-wall but her class understand the idea of investing in the drama (building commitment) and they therefore respond readily to what promises to be a far more exciting activity.

She reminds them of Mars the Roman god of war and asks them to imagine a statue to a typical soldier erected in one of his temples. In twos they should think not only of a quality but a couple of sentences telling an anecdote that illustrates the quality, e.g. 'A Roman soldier is untiring. He marches for a whole day with a sixty-pound pack on his back.' Some pairs use a historical fact – Horatius defending the bridge for example. Others say something more personal: 'Our friend Marcellus died heroically in battle.' They write their sentence(s) on a 'laurel crown' made from a simple circle of paper. A volunteer is sought to be the statue and he or she is arranged by the class into a suitable pose. All the ingredients of the scene are now ready.

Terri takes the role of the priest of the temple and in a ceremony with the rituals decided communally each pair places their laurel wreath in a position round the statue, formally pronouncing what is written on it as they do so. Terri sets the scene and keeps it on course with suitable heightened language, starting the whole thing off by lighting two candles which volunteer acolytes set on either side of the statue. Three children use percussion instruments to mark the beginning of the ceremony and the moments when the wreaths are laid. The whole activity is marked by a sense of solemnity and they all treat it with utter seriousness. In fact, in this case, some of the class at the end are dissatisfied with certain of the details and suggest better ways of doing it. These suggestions are incorporated and the ceremony is performed again.

The first session ends here

3   Terri performs a monologue, introducing herself as Flavius, a young Roman who longs to be a soldier. 'He' is from a good family and has a wife and a young baby. (Terri plants this latter fact because she plans to use it later in the drama.) 'He' continues by explaining that he has had lots of different advice: some people have advised him to do it, others have warned him against it. (As usual when doing such monologues Terri uses heightened language to capture the children's imaginations and she doesn't give too much away in order to make them work.)

Terri then comes out of role and says that she would like to enact these scenes and asks how they could do it. After some discussion, they decide that they will take on group roles positioned about the room and that Flavius will approach them one at a time to ask their advice. They decide who they will be and someone suggests that Flavius should approach people in various ways: he will not be the same with his mates in the tavern as with his wife or with a distinguished senator he knows. After a couple of minutes to get their ideas together, Terri starts. Flavius goes from one group to another taking advice, but not content just to listen in silence, he argues, moving away from one group to an opposing one, getting *its* advice which he then brings back to the first group. Thus a lively debate ensues and passions are aroused. It is controlled because Terri can move away from a group that becomes too vociferous to a quieter one with a different point of view.

This part of the drama is based on the drama convention conscience alley which has been adapted and expanded to fit the particular circumstances required (see Unit 4).

4   Out of role, Terri then narrates a further episode of the story. Flavius went to ask advice of one of the priests in the temple of Mars who advised that he should spend the night alone in the temple praying to the god for guidance. This he did and during the night Mars appeared to him and spoke. He showed him visions of the glories of war, of heroic exploits and the honours that would be heaped upon him.

Once again Terri asks the class how they should enact this. They decide that Flavius should see mimed actions which demonstrate the glories that Mars talks about. Terri agrees but asks them first to make three still images showing the beginning, the middle and the end of the mime. They can then go on to constructing the bits in between the images. (This is part of a general scheme she is pursuing to help them understand structure.) She also asks them to consider whereabouts they will be in relation to Flavius when they perform their mime. Will they be distant from him? Hovering over him? Moving round him? (In other words she is asking them to consider spatial relationships.) They also decide in which order the mimes should occur. In the end the class ask her to take the role of Flavius (he doesn't have to do much!) while a volunteer plays Mars and directs the scene through the role. The girl taking the part of Mars needs some help at first with appropriate language to start the scene and provide suitable links but others help her out and in the end she does rather well.

The scene concludes with Flavius making up his mind to join the Roman army.

The second session ends here

5   For the next lesson, Terri has to make a decision. She senses that the class want to get on with what they would regard as a story. She could spend another whole period of time on Flavius's army training and 'passing out' but decides to shorten the proceedings and instead do a whole-group narration. As part of their learning about Roman history they have done a lot on the Roman army so they are acquainted with the details of what would have happened. They also know from their small group monologues the technique of speaking at random and picking up the threads of the narrative from one another. So far, however, they have never done it as a whole class. She asks them to stand together in a tight phalanx as if they were Roman soldiers, with a space in the middle of the front row. Flavius (a volunteer-in-role) stands facing them as far away as possible and as the narration proceeds he gets nearer and nearer until finally he joins the ranks. The Centurian (another volunteer) calls the group to attention and they then march forward a few steps as if starting off on a campaign. Terri acts as a facilitator for this scene, standing outside the action, helping and advising. It takes a number of run-throughs to get it right but eventually it is done to everyone's satisfaction.

6   Terri now comes out of role, gathers the class round her and more or less puts her cards on

the table. She tells them she wants Flavius to be part of the invading army to Britain but during the journey and during the time in Britain before the main battle (a scene from which they've already done), she wants him gradually to change his views – to find things different from how Mars presented them in the temple. She asks first of all what sort of things could have happened to make him change. Suggestions are made: the hardship of his life; missing his wife and baby; people who are themselves starving helping him; seeing people being butchered senselessly; seeing a young family like his own without a father; seeing his colleagues wounded, maimed and blinded; wondering *why* they are going on this campaign to capture a remote island that nobody cares about.

As is customary Terri asks how they are going to represent these ideas in drama. After much discussion, someone suggests that they should have Flavius before the main battle in Britain, remembering events that have happened to him and things he has seen. Some events will be just still images, some will be enacted scenes, some will be groups who come and talk to him – 'in his mind sort of …'. In the enactment of these episodes, where Terri plays the role of Flavius remembering, she sets up a refrain, 'Why am I here, what's it all for?'

7   Terri then asks them if one couple will once again enact the fight between Flavius and the Prince and she will take the drama forward and play the 'thing' that froze his blood. She will just do a minute or two of the drama after which she'll stop. They can then decide to alter it or take it on further in the way they want. They agree to help her to build up an atmosphere by a sound picture using voices, percussion instruments and so on – firstly to accompany the fight and secondly to depict the mystery that follows. Meanwhile Terri has enlisted the help of two girls who will help her in her role. They will appear to Flavius as the three ancient shrouded Mother Goddesses, carvings of which have been found in several places in Britain. They will walk either side of her holding their hands as if carrying the large eggs depicted in the carvings, and as such being representative of life and fertility. She produces some long pieces of material (jumble-sale stuff) which they all drape round their heads and shoulders.

They begin the scene with the class gathered round the two fighters. The three Mother Goddesses enter from behind, walking through the class and confronting Flavius. Terri makes a short speech outlining that she is a goddess of life while Flavius follows the god of death and destruction. She tells him that the Prince that he is about to kill has a wife and a baby like him and points out the misery and suffering that have been caused by the Roman army. She ends by asking him to lay down his weapon and join with the Prince in following her.

8   The drama is stopped and Terri asks the question: should Flavius kill the Prince or do what the Mother Goddesses want? A lively discussion starts immediately and she uses it to tease out some of the problems associated with either course of action. One of these is the fact that not only would a Roman soldier convicted of cowardice be executed himself but so too would every tenth man in his legion. Another problem is what the Prince says as he is about to be killed: 'Oh Mother Goddess, protect my wife and baby daughter.'

9   The final scene as devised by the class consists of the fight, followed by the appearance of the Mother Goddesses followed by a spirited rejoinder from Mars (the girl who played him earlier). There then follows the appearance of a number of characters, some who have appeared already in the drama, others (like the Prince's aged father) who have not.

In the end Flavius does kill the Prince but he does it sorrowfully and kneels by his body for some time afterwards. The rest of the class watches in silence until the Mother Goddesses turn and move slowly away....

10   The children reflect on the drama by imagining Flavius many years later, now a successful commander in the Roman army, visiting the tomb of the Prince. Terri in role as Flavius approaches a chair representing the tomb while the children, sitting in a circle, narrate the thoughts that are going through his head.

There are two elements of theatre which straddle this Unit and the previous one and so it seems appropriate to deal with them first. Both were identified by the critic and writer William Archer in his classic book *Play-Making* (1912). The first element he calls the *obligatory scene* and he defines it as 'one which the audience ... foresees and desires, and the absence of which it may with reason resent'. Plainly it is important to recognize this in a drama lesson in school because it can be a useful tool in keeping interest alive. The promise of doing the scene that they all 'foresee and desire' will sugar the pill of other scenes that the teacher thinks important but which the children may not immediately find appealing. The obligatory scene often occurs at the climax of the lesson – but not always. In the drama you have just read it is the fight between Flavius and the Prince – including the outcome. You will note how cunningly Terri places a portion of it at the beginning with the promise that they will return to it at the end – a device which is also popular with the makers of

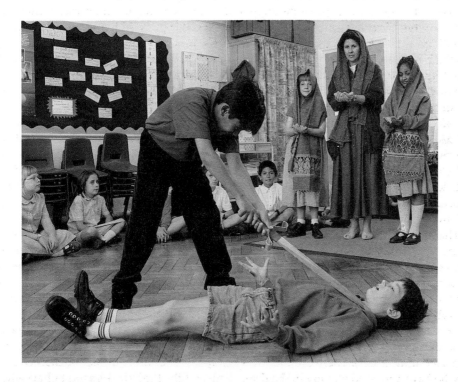

Plate 11 Enacting the battle while the Mother Goddesses look on

television drama. It is also useful to note that the obligatory scene does not necessarily have to be *played* and indeed it might not be appropriate to do so. The rape of the Sabine women or the total destruction of a tribe of native American Indians by white settlers in your drama lesson might be the scenes the class desperately wants to see but letting them be acted out could lead to all kinds of problems! They can be replaced instead with a narration by the teacher, either in role as a character in the drama or out of role simply as 'the narrator'. Those of us who think this is simply a cop-out or might result in a weakening of the drama only have to look at the powerful tragedies of Ancient Greece to see how *they* used such devices to great effect.

The second of Archer's theatrical elements is described by a word from the Greek theatre – peripeteia or in its Anglicized version, 'peripety'. In general terms it means some change or reversal of fortune within the drama. Archer extends this by saying that it involves a great scene where one or more of the characters 'experience a marked reversal either of inward soul state or of outward fortune'. It can be fairly crude where, for example, someone suddenly loses all his or her money or it can be more subtle, as (we hope) in the Roman drama where Flavius experiences a change of heart in his attitude towards war. Notwithstanding this, however it is used, it is an extremely useful theatrical weapon to have at your disposal and will help to make your drama more successful.

 ACTIVITY 6.1

Obligatory scene and peripeteia

1   Go through the dramas outlined in this book and identify the obligatory scenes. If you were going to teach the dramas consider how you could make them different – e.g. put the obligatory scene in a different place, change its state from narration to enactment or vice versa. What effect would this have on the dramas? Would it make them better or worse?

   (Don't be afraid to change things. We are not claiming that the dramas we have devised are perfect.)

2   Look over the dramas and identify instances of peripeteia. Again could you alter the dramas to make these more obvious, more effective? Consider what effect such a change would have in relation to the children you teach.

   (In devising dramas for this book we have in mind children we have taught – but *your* children might require something different – something simpler, more complex, more obvious, more sophisticated. Modify accordingly.)

Most people when they think of 'theatrical elements' have in mind the immediately visible parts of the theatre – a set, lights, costumes and so on. We will be considering these later in the Unit but as we have said earlier, they are not the most important in respect of our drama lessons in school. Indeed, they can become so intrusive that they positively detract from the drama's effectiveness.

What *is* important, however, and without which your drama lesson simply will not work, is **theatrical tension**. In fact, in the film *Three Looms Waiting*, Dorothy Heathcote goes as far as saying 'put the tension there and the rest of the drama will follow'. A number of other writers have also had comments to make about it, among them Gavin Bolton (1979) and Norah Morgan and Juliana Saxton (1987). The common conception of tension in theatrical or dramatic terms is what we would term 'suspense'.

> A policeman searches through a silent warehouse for the unhinged, escaped criminal – the audience knows he is hiding, armed to the teeth but like the policeman we don't know where. Usually on film and television music helps the suspense which continues until the criminal leaps out accompanied by frenzied screaming on the violins.

That kind of situation certainly does contain tension but at its most extreme. Normally it is far more low-key. Bolton (1979) defines it as 'in inequilibrium' while Morgan and Saxton (1987) describe it more usefully as 'mental excitement'. Furthermore these two authors divide it into seven aspects that have become generally accepted: Time, Unknown, Constraint, Challenge, Evaluation, Responsibility and Space. We have placed them in a sequence so that the first letter of each spells the mnemonic, TUCCERS.

- *Time*

  This concerns any situation where time is limited. Our (faulty) memory of the original *Star Trek* series is that every episode ended with Mr Scott the engineer working frantically to repair the ship against a time limit (shown by a clock ticking away on screen). He always completed the task at the very last second, just as the ship was about to be blown up, dematerialized or whatever. In a drama lesson we might say, 'The first rays of the sun will strike the bridge at any minute. We have to get across this bridge without attracting the guards' attention before it does.' This does not have the frenzy of *Star Trek* but it engenders that extra bit of mental excitement that would not be present if we said 'We've got to get across the bridge.'

- *Unknown*

  In horror movies, the unknown evil presence is always more terrifying than when we actually see the monster for ourselves, partly because our imagination works for us but also because we don't know what it is like but we want to. Anything that makes the children want to know something will work in the same way. Produce a box or a bag and they will want to know what is inside it. Produce a coded letter and they will be interested in deciphering it. Even leaving a vital piece of information until the end of the speech will have the same effect e.g. 'You have all been chosen for this mission because you have one quality in common. As I've spoken to you in your interviews I've noticed it. And in the mission we are about to go on it is vital to our success. I'm speaking of course about your ability to keep calm under stress.'

- *Constraint*

  In the *Inspector Morse* series on television, on a number of occasions Morse's superior takes him off the case he is working on before he has finished his investigations. If he wishes to continue (which of course he does) he must do so with the constraint of working undercover without the normal police back-up. In playwrighting terms this is so that he doesn't reach his conclusion too quickly and from the audience's point of view it provides more interest and 'mental excitement'. Will he solve the crime with these obstacles in his path? Placing obstacles in the way of solving the dramatic problem too easily and quickly is also a key weapon in the drama teacher's armoury. It is also useful on a smaller scale. Notice that in the section on Time above, as well as moving quickly the children were provided with the constraint of moving unnoticed. There would have been little tension if they had been encouraged to rush across the bridge in a Gadarene stampede!

- *Challenge*
  Many dramas are based on a challenge: catching the thief, finding the jewels, rescuing the princess. Smaller challenges can be included within the overall structure, however. For example, getting across the bridge unnoticed before the sun comes up involves the tension of Challenge as well as Constraint and Time.

- *Evaluation*
  The essence of Inspector Morse's job is to evaluate one piece of evidence against another. He must apply judgement and in doing so, we as the audience are taken along with him. Similarly in the classroom, ask the children to decide whether *this* course of action is better than *that* and you have the tension of evaluation. (They are also of course, *challenged* to find the best one.)

- *Responsibility*
  Many dramas are driven by the fact of the central character's responsibility. Referring to Inspector Morse once more it is frequently his sense of responsibility to the victim or the victim's family that forces him to continue, even when he has been ordered to abandon the case by his superior. In a school drama we could, for example, create a sense of tension by endowing responsibility on the villagers not to reveal the whereabouts of the fugitive when the soldiers come looking for him or her.

- *Space*
  In many ways this element is the odd one out because it refers to the actual physical positions of the actors in the drama. Generally speaking, the more confined the space is, the greater the sense of tension will be – although this could also be seen as Constraint. It is an easy tension to forget – we have found ourselves on occasions in a drama lesson talking to the children in the physical positions that they happen to find themselves in, rather than working at the spatial arrangement until it feels right.

Other practitioners have their own favourite tensions not included in the Morgan and Saxton list. Secrecy is a popular one and is certainly effective – although, like others it can be subsumed under the tension of Constraint. Whoever holds the secret is constrained not to tell it.

Given our practice in the rest of the book, you could be forgiven for thinking that what now follows will be an activity asking you to identify these tensions in one or more of the dramas outlined in the book. Indeed it would be perfectly possible to do such an activity. Yet we hesitate…

The tensions as described are important – and as we have shown in the examples, they do exist and they do work. But in our practice we have noticed that we have only ever identified them *after* the drama is over. We've done something and then said 'That worked well. Oh yes, it was because it contained the tension of the unknown' or 'I wonder why that didn't work? Oh, of course, it didn't contain any tension. We should have, say, put a time limit on the action to tighten things up.' Even in planning we have tended to think of a situation or event first and then realise what type of tension it is afterwards. This ties in with the fact, as we have indicated in our descriptions above, that many of the tensions appear to overlap and indeed, we can actually include them all under one heading – Constraint.

The Morgan and Saxton categories also don't account in any useful way for the sense of theatrical tension a teacher can engender by the way he or she behaves and the attitude and tone of voice that is adopted. For example, take the narration that the teacher makes at the end of Section 1 of *The Roman Soldier* which accompanies the fight between Flavius and the Prince. The amount of tension engendered at that point will depend very much on how the teacher does the narration. It could be dull and flat or electric in intensity.

So what does all this mean for someone who's got to teach a drama lesson tomorrow? It means three things:

1   While you are actually teaching the drama you can keep in your head one thing instead of seven. Think **Constraint**. Just as playwrights place obstacles in the path of their characters to stop them from solving the problem too easily, so the teacher places constraints on the characters and situations in the drama for the same reason.

2   A successful teacher of drama has to have a sense of **theatricality**. You should be able to be a bit 'over-the-top'.

(Now before you throw this book aside, saying 'Being a luvvie is not my style' – wait! We're going to go further into the idea of theatricality in a minute. It's not what you think!)

3   A sense of **energy** is needed, by which we don't mean you have to throw yourself frantically round the classroom. Rather it means a seriousness, a commitment and a single-mindedness, particularly when taking a role or, say, setting a scene through narration.

KEY POINTS

Tension is vital to successful drama.

It can be divided into Time, Unknown, Constraint, Challenge, Evaluation, Responsibility and Space. All these can be subsumed under **Constraint**.

Tension in *performance* can be achieved by **energy** and a sense of **theatricality**.

ACTIVITY 6.2

Constraint

Look over *The Roman Soldier* drama.

Identify each place where Terri puts a **constraint** on either the characters or situation.

If you were teaching this drama to your class, imagine at each of these stages how *you* would put this constraint into practice.

ACTIVITY 6.3

Theatricality (Part A)

Look at Section 1 of *The Roman Soldier*.

Write down the brief narrative that accompanies the fight scene. Try to write it in a heightened way, using evocative words and images, particularly towards the end when Flavius sees something coming towards him.

Now think about how you might perform the narrative. Think about where you will stand, what position you will be in, where you will look. Will you move? What will you do with your hands? How will you create a sense of energy? By the use of your voice? gestures?

Now perform this narrative out loud (in private). If necessary hold the script that you have written, but above all *feel* that you are creating the scene for the children. *You* are responsible for capturing their interest through *what* you say and *how* you say it.

Let's now look further at this notion of theatricality. We mentioned in Unit 4 that drama in school works best if it is not based on realism and, indeed, realism has dogged the British theatre (and the theatre of the West generally for that matter). Ask the person in the street about a play and they will judge it for the most part from the point of view of how close to real life it is. It is difficult for us to appreciate that this is not what other cultures do (nor our culture before the middle of the nineteenth century). All the great theatres of the world have used a theatrical language that is not judged from the point of view of everyday 'real' life. And it is this language which gives the theatre its power.

We also mentioned earlier, in our discussion of role, how it can be viewed as a system of signs and rather than look at a drama as an imitation of reality, it is far more useful to look at drama and theatre as a whole – the way signals are conveyed to an audience. Much complex analysis has been made in this area recently (see Aston and Savona 1991), but plainly stated whatever we see on stage we see as a signal of something more than simply what it is. We look for a *meaning*. A story will illustrate how it works. A friend of ours went to see an amateur production of Shakespeare's *Twelfth Night*. On the set, towards the front of the stage, was a large basket of flowers which stayed there throughout and being a student of drama our friend puzzled over these for the whole of the performance. What were they meant to indicate? Joy? Spring? The force of life through nature? It was only afterwards that she discovered they had been placed there by a well-wisher in the audience to wish the cast good luck.

Theatrical signs can operate in a range of ways from the simple to the obvious. Looking at the simple first, in the theatre nowadays we often see a skeleton set – a free-standing door and a window suspended on wires for example. This signals to the audience the idea of 'a room'. We don't need all the realistic trappings of fireplaces, solid-looking walls and so on. We've already considered how in classroom drama a teacher will often use something fairly straightforward to signify the role he or she is taking. A headscarf can sign a peasant woman; a clipboard or briefcase, an official of

Plate 12 Prince Flavius – here the teacher has used a range of theatrical elements to enhance the drama

some sort; a crown, a king or a queen. Words or gestures can also be used in such a way. For example in the drama at the beginning of the chapter the judicious use of one or two specialist words such as *castrum* (meaning fortress) or *legate* (a high ranking army officer) will sign the idea of 'Roman' simply and effectively, as will a well-chosen gesture such as the army salute with fist clenched and arm across the chest.

These devices are used because they capture some important essence about the role or the scene quickly and efficiently but the danger is that they can easily lapse into stereotypes – conveying only a simple and often misleading shorthand set of messages (a frilly apron signalling 'Mum' for instance). Good theatre, however, works at a richer and more complex level with the signs not only conveying a simple message but having wider implications or *resonances*. With the question of objects, as a drama teacher it is often a matter of looking around for things that have a resonance contained within them. On holiday in Tunisia we bought very cheaply a leather draw-string purse which when suitably distressed with dark boot polish looked like a bag from ancient times which could contain some kind of treasure. Similarly, on another holiday we picked up a small glass perfume bottle, decorated with metal filigree work and glass beads which has provided an evocative container for a precious elixir of life used in one of our dramas. A piece of scrunched-up red velvet curtain on which rests the 'sword of state' (borrowed from a local amateur theatre company's stock cupboard) has a far greater resonance of significance and 'kingliness' than the sword by itself plonked on a table.

In the school drama *Susie and the Snow*, mentioned in the last Unit, Judith Ackroyd narrates the sequence where Susie skates up the frozen river, falls through the ice and is then rescued. When we saw the drama the children were standing in a circle. As she performed the narrative, Ackroyd took a coat belonging to one of the class and as she came to the point where Susie had fallen into the river and was holding onto the ice she bundled the coat up carefully, placed it on the floor in the centre of the circle and spread the arms out wide. As she reached the point where at last Susie is rescued, she carefully gathered the coat up, cradled it in her arms and walked away from the children. In this case the coat signalled 'Susie fallen in the river' and 'Susie being rescued' far more powerfully than if she had tried to do it 'realistically' with a real child. Just as importantly however is the *way* Ackroyd performed the actions, slowly and with attention and seriousness. You can imagine that if she had done it with embarrassment or too quickly, or if her voice had had a level of flippancy, the effect would have been marred. In other words, the signs are only as good as the teacher who uses them.

KEY POINTS

Good drama works through **signs** rather than a straightforward imitation of real life.

The best signs are ones which have **resonance** – they imply more than what they obviously stand for.

The way the teacher signs is just as important as the signs themselves.

ACTIVITY 6.4

Theatricality (Part B)

First of all look at Section 2 of *The Roman Soldier* drama at the beginning of the Unit. Identify the signs that are mentioned during the description (e.g. the candles and the laurel wreaths). With each one of them, try to identify what they are signing and what some of the resonances could be.

Plan how exactly you would 'stage' this scene if you were to do it with your class, and particularly what signs you would use in your own role to convey the role of 'priest'. Words? Gestures? Significant pieces of costume or props?

For as long as we have been dealing with teachers and drama-in-education we've noticed that the teachers who do it best are those who have some idea about theatre and the way it works. What often happens is that such teachers frequently don't realize intellectually how it's done, they seem to just do it instinctively. We have hoped in this Unit to show something of the 'nuts and bolts' of theatricality and, particularly, that you don't have to be an actor or an actress to make it work for you and the children in your class. What you do have to do is to know about tension and signing and when you 'perform' do it with utter seriousness – as if you really believe in the role you are portraying.

With this in mind, we come to the final exercise.

 ACTIVITY 6.5

Theatricality (Part C)

Look back to the drama you created in Unit 5, the one we entitled *A Traveller called Danny*

Rework the plan in terms of:

a) Tension: does it have tension built in to the structure? If it doesn't, how could you alter it? In what ways could you contribute to the tension by the way you teach the lesson?
b) Signs: how are you signing? Could it be improved? How could what you have learned about theatricality enhance the drama?

In this book we have shown the work of three fictitious teachers. One of them, Terri, represents our ideal: she teaches the dramas that in our best moments, occasionally, when the stars were right, when everything gelled together just as it should, we have taught! Another, Derek, represents how we have taught in the past – and when we've got other things on our mind or we've got a headache or the kids are playing up, we teach still. Chris is the person we would like to think we really are: getting it right for a lot of the time – but open to new ideas and still learning. All three teachers, however, are giving the kids in their care the chance of that marvellous experience where their ideas come to life in drama. So whether you identify with Derek, Chris or Terri, we do hope that you will put into practice some of the things we've outlined in this book. *We* believe it is more than worthwhile and we think that you will find it so too. Good luck!

Appendix I   Key Stage 2 programme of study

Pupils' abilities should be developed within an integrated programme of speaking and listening, reading and writing. Pupils should be given opportunities that interrelate the requirements of the Range, Key Skills and Standard English and Language Study sections.

Speaking and Listening

1.   Range

a   Pupils should be given opportunities to talk for a range of purposes, including:

> exploring, developing and explaining ideas;
> planning, predicting and investigating;
> sharing ideas, insights and opinions;
> reading aloud, telling and enacting stories and poems;
> reporting and describing events and observations;
> presenting to audiences, live or on tape.

b   Pupils should be given opportunities to communicate to different audiences and to reflect on how speakers adapt their vocabulary, tone, pace and style.

c   Pupils should be given opportunities to listen and respond to a range of people. They should be taught to identify and comment on key features of what they see and hear in a variety of media.

d   Pupils should be given opportunities to participate in a wide range of drama activities, including improvisation, role-play and the writing and performance of scripted drama. In responding to drama, they should be encouraged to evaluate their own and others' contributions.

2. Key Skills

a   Pupils should be encouraged to express themselves confidently and clearly. Pupils should be taught to organize what they want to say and to use vocabulary and syntax that enables the communication of more complex meanings. In discussions, pupils should be given opportunities to make a range of contributions, depending on the activity and the purpose of the talk. This range should include making exploratory and tentative comments when ideas are being collected together and making reasoned, evaluative comments as discussion moves to conclusions or action. Pupils should be taught to evaluate their own talk and reflect on how it varies.

b   Pupils should be taught to listen carefully and to recall and re-present important features of an argument, talk, presentation, reading, radio or television programme. They should be taught to identify the gist of an account or the key points made in discussion, to evaluate what they hear and to make contributions that are relevant to what is being considered. They should be taught to listen to others, questioning them to clarify what they mean and extending and following up the ideas. They should be encouraged to qualify or justify what they think after listening to other opinions or accounts and deal politely with opposing points of view.

3.   Standard English and Language Study

a   Pupils' appreciation and use of standard English should be developed by involvement with others in activities that, through their content and purpose, demand the range of grammatical constructions and vocabulary characteristic of spoken standard English. They should be taught to speak with clear diction and appropriate intonation. Pupils should be taught how formal contexts require particular choices of vocabulary and greater precision in language structures. They should also be given opportunities to develop their understanding of the similarities and differences between the written and spoken forms of standard English and to investigate how language varies according to context and purpose and between standard and dialect forms.

b   Pupils should be taught to use an increasingly varied vocabulary. The range of pupils' vocabulary should be extended and enriched through activities that focus on words and their meanings, including:

> discussion of more imaginative and adventurous choices of words;
> consideration of groups of words, *e.g. word families, the range of words*
> *relevant to a topic;*
> language used in drama, role-play and word games.

Appendix II   Extracts from key writers on drama in education

AN INTRODUCTION TO CHILD DRAMA, **PETER SLADE (1958)**

 What would you expect to find in good Child Drama lessons?

They should be joyful, in an encouraging atmosphere. The teacher should be keen, quiet, kindly, observant, and know how to stimulate if necessary. There should be variety and new creation, clear defined shapes in movement and good use of space. Questions should be answered adequately, suggestion encouraged and used. There should be complete control, with good contrast – noise and quiet. Speech should be flowing, rapid and unhesitating, of poetic and philosophic language between six and ten, and increasingly witty and gay between ten and fifteen. There should be zest in the acting, good group sensitivity, marked sincerity and absorption, bringing high moments of 'theatre'. I would hope to see things, animals, people or movements I had not thought of, and an example of 'running play'. The unconscious grouping would be exciting. Everybody would get an equal chance of creation.

That would be a pretty good lesson. The teacher would not teach, but guide and nurture; he, too, has to be a creative artist, constantly ready to offer aid if needed.

There are no short cuts to this work, no hard or easy rules. Each child is different, each teacher learns to handle things his own way. Before starting we must love the child, love the work, and know why we do it. If we cannot at all times love, because of tiredness, then we must develop a deep sense of justice. For at the root of all creative opportunity lies an elementary justice for the child. Together with the child a wisdom is built, and an emotional sharing experienced. Out of this grows the indefinable knowledge of life that constitutes for the child *education* in the full sense of the word.

(pp. 84–85)

EDUCATION IN DRAMA, DAVID HORNBROOK (1991)

Because it is a way of making better sense of things (what has been called elsewhere, 'a way of knowing'), art, like religion, is also a form of usefulness. Not because it offers us amusement, easy recognition, a way of escaping from reality – usefulness in the sense I employ it here is not to be confused with convenience or utility – but because with its religious antecedents, it helps to explain the world and to show us how we should live. When what professes to be art is not useful – when it is empty of meaning, or repetitive, or nothing more than shallow imitation – then it can no longer have a purchase on our lives.

When, on the other hand, art moves us and engages us deeply, it is because it is rooted in the sensibility of a culture to which we belong. That sensibility is itself informed by the signs and metaphors of residual belief which remain in culture as shadows, or traces, inherited by the very language we speak and through which we make ourselves understood. Genuine engagement with art is thus a form of aesthetic recognition, an experience which in modern societies is as likely to disturb as confirm, illuminating paradoxes and leading us to new interpretations and greater enlightenment. Art is useful not because it is true but because it is truly edifying.

It is because drama-as-art functions in this way that a dramatic work cannot be explained, paraphrased or deconstructed into a series of essays. Like any other art form, drama is unique and non-convertible. Although plays may be interpreted by painters or composers, as in Prokofiev's *Romeo and Juliet*, for example, drama cannot be *translated* into paintings or music so that the one can be said to stand for the other. Like a primary colour in the arts spectrum, drama is reducible only to itself. Similarly, however challenging or illuminating, drama is not of necessity a means to any end, however worthy, beyond itself. It resists crassly utilitarian efforts to corral it into the service of geography, history or management training as much as it refuses to be the acquiescent servant of personal, social, or political education. In a secular age, the usefulness of drama lies in its ability to articulate meaning in particularly direct and accessible ways so that we, in turn, can make better sense of the world in which we live. For these reasons, drama is an indispensable part of the arts curriculum.

(pp. 40–41)

TOWARDS A THEORY OF DRAMA IN EDUCATION, GAVIN BOLTON (1979)

At last we have reached the central point of this book: that drama in education is primarily concerned with change in appraisal, an affective/cognitive develop-ment. We can conveniently refer it is as 'Drama for understanding': this is what the teacher is teaching and the learner is learning. We shall be examining this 'learning area' in different ways in subsequent chapters. It will suffice here to give a few illustrations to clarify the kind of concept with which we are most concerned.

Because drama operates subjectively and objectively the learning is related to those concepts about which value judgments are made. The kind of important learning that deliberately discourages value judgments (for example, the classification of animals into vertebrates and non-vertebrates) is best acquired, in my opinion, through modes other than drama. On the other hand a concept such as 'Progress relies on people taking risks' might be understood differently if the learner is subjected to the experiential mode of drama. Most concepts can have both kinds of orientation. Take the concept of 'protection': an evolutionist or a zoologist may examine different ways in which animals do or do not protect their young; a sociologist may similarly research protection of one generation by another among human beings. But 'protection' as a concept can also connote a whole range of personal meanings that stem from the user's affective life. It is these meanings that drama can most carefully open up for the participants. As educationalists we have failed to appreciate this dual orientation. We have assumed that pedagogy is the training of children in the neutral observation of objective facts. Teachers have often only paid lip-service to, or ignored, the affective orientation or, equally mistakenly, have assumed that such an orientation means free expression rather than understanding. In my view, both orientations are directed towards the development of concepts and we have a responsibilty to make both modes available to the children we teach.

(pp. 38–39)

DEVELOPMENT THROUGH DRAMA, BRIAN WAY (1967)

The most important single factor in the use of drama as a genuine part of education is the teacher. It would be preposterous to pretend that a teacher needs no preparation for doing drama – but it is equally preposterous to suggest that a teacher who sees the values of using drama needs a course in theatre. A really full, generous and compassionate interest in children, irrespective of academic ability or gifts, is the first requisite; a knowledge of why to use drama is another; the freedom to approach the matter from where he or she feels happiest and most confident is another. For the latter reason, many rules and conventions, both of drama and of teaching, may have to be ignored. (After all, rules are made for mankind, not mankind for rules.) Thus, as already mentioned, it may be wisest to start with the three or five minute lesson; it may be necessary to begin a drama lesson with, say, 'difficult' fifteen-year-old boys by a discussion of the Tottenham Hotspur's XI, or, with similar girls, to discuss hair-styles or dating boy friends. These subject matters are a far cry from the so-called progressive rules of drama – (e.g. start with movement and progress to speech), but are entirely relevant if our basic premise is that of developing people rather than drama. By the same token, a book such as this can be a positive menace! The book itself must contain a certain degree of form, and its form may suggest a factor of progression which is entirely erroneous and unintended. For any teacher who may find some help from the practical suggestions put forward, I would add the thought: 'Start from where you yourself are happiest and most confident; this may be the telling of a story or it may be a simple discussion about appropriate behaviour in certain situations; it may be the problems of the school play or a discussion on Hamlet's attitude to Claudius; it may be a deep concern with teaching Christian charity or simply asking someone to take a telephone message; it may be a simple concern with sharing physical space and material objects or the complex understanding of racial problems. Start from that point – from where you yourself feel interested and confident. Keep reminding yourself that what you are concerned with is the development of every one of the manifold facets of human beings; a circle can start at any point on the circumference of that circle. Ultimately there may be only one goal, but the means to that goal are manifold and individual, depending on where you, as teacher, are, and growing out of the particular bond you have made with the children or young people you are helping to develop.

But to develop people we need to start by considering some aspects of the basic nature of human beings; whatever practical manner we find for beginning drama, these basic aspects of humanity are relevant.

(pp. 8–9)

DOROTHY HEATHCOTE: DRAMA AS A LEARNING MEDIUM, BETTY-JANE WAGNER (1979)

Wherever Heathcote goes, she generates excitement and even adulation. She emanates power. Her power is like that of a *medium*, bringing into the present the distant in time or space, making it come alive in our consciousness through imagined group experience. This awareness stands in contrast to the effect of the mass news *media* which bring us the contemporary in time but often leave it still distant in space and remote to our sense. The plethora of stimuli that bombards us through the media deadens our responsiveness. Because there is too much coming too fast to make sense of emotionally, our feelings are seldom touched. With the artist's sensitivity, Heathcote slows the input of information, eliminates the irrelevant, and selects the single symbol that can evoke the widest range of meanings; then she lets it slowly do its work, unravelling response within each student; she never tells a student what to feel or think, never pushes for more than the student can discover independently.

This does not mean that Dorothy Heathcote doesn't press children. She does; and this is perhaps one of her most controversial techniques. Creative drama teachers in America are sometimes critical of her pressures to achieve dramatic focus, her deliberate upgrading of language, her insistence on slowing pace to allow for reflection and inner awareness. In this respect, again, she is like a medium. A spell has to be cast; rituals must be followed; conditions have to be right; the universal inherent in this moment must be realised, and she's witch like in her control leading to this effect. She arrests attention, wins commitment, magnetises, combining both a wildness and a control in her work. She works with children with authority, intuition, and a thorough understanding of the potential and limits of drama.

She does not use children to produce plays. Instead, she uses drama to expand their awareness, to enable them to look at reality through fantasy, to see below the surface of actions to their meaning. She is interested, not in making plays with children, but in, as she terms it, burnishing children through the play. She does this not by heaping more information on them but by enabling them to use what they already know.

(pp. 14–15)

Appendix III Annotated extract from *Richard III*, Act V, Scene iii, William Shakespeare

Enter the Ghost of Prince Edward, son to Henry the Sixth.

> Ghost.   Let me sit heavy on thy soul tomorrow!
> Think how thou stab'st me in my prime of youth
> At Tewkesbury. Despair therefor and die!...

Enter the Ghost of Henry the Sixth.

> Ghost.   When I was mortal, my anointed body
> By thee was punchèd full of deadly holes.
> Think on the Tower and me. Despair and die!
> Harry the Sixth bids thee despair and die!...

Enter the Ghost of Clarence.

> Ghost.   Let me sit heavy in thy soul tomorrow,
> I that was washed to death with fulsome wine,
> Poor Clarence, by thy guile betrayed to death.
> Tomorrow in the battle think on me,
> And fall thy edgeless sword. Despair and die!...

Enter the Ghosts of Rivers, Grey and Vaughan.

> Rivers.   Let me sit heavy in thy soul tomorrow,
> Rivers, that died at Pomfret! Despair and die!
> Grey   Think upon Grey, and let thy soul despair!
> Vaughan.   Think upon Vaughan and with guilty fear
> Let fall thy lance: despair, and die!...

Enter the Ghost of Hastings.

Ghost.   Bloody and guilty, guiltily awake,
                 And in a bloody battle end thy days!
                 Think on Lord Hastings. Despair and die!...

Enter the Ghosts of the two young Princes.

Ghosts.   Dream on thy cousins smother'ed in the tower.
                 Let us be laid within thy bosom, Richard,
                 And weigh thee down to ruin, shame, and death.
                 Thy nephews' souls bid thee despair and die!...

Enter the Ghost of Lady Anne his wife.

Ghost.   Richard, thy wife, that wretched Anne thy wife,
                 That never slept a quiet hour with thee,
                 Now fills thy sleep with perturbations.
                 Tomorrow in the battle think on me,.
                 And fall thy edgeless sword. Despair and die!...

Enter the Ghost of Buckingham.

Ghost.   The first was I That helped thee to the crown;
                 The last was I that felt thy tyranny.
                 O, in the battle think on Buckingham,
                 And die in terror of thy guiltiness!
                 Dream on, dream on, of bloody deeds and death;
                 Fainting, despair; despairing, yield thy breath!

Source: *The Signet Classic Shakespeare* (1964), London: The New English Library Ltd.

Bibliography

Ackroyd, J. (1994) 'A crack in the ice', *Language and Learning* November/December, pp. 27–30.

Archer, W. (1912) *Play-Making. A Manual of Craftsmanship*, London: Chapman & Hall.

Aston, E. and Savona, G. (1991) *Theatre as a sign system*, London: Routledge.

BBC (1970) *Three Looms Waiting*.

Best, D. (1985) *Feeling and Reason in the Arts*, London: George Allen and Unwin.

Best, D. (1992) *The Rationality of Feeling*, London: The Falmer Press.

Blank-Grief, E. (1976) 'Sex role playing in pre-school children', in J. S. Bruner, A. Jolly and K. Sylva (eds) *Play*, Harmondsworth: Penguin Books.

Bolton, G. (1979) *Towards a Theory of Drama in Education*, Harlow: Longman.

Brook, P. (1990) *The Empty Space*, Harmondsworth: Penguin.

Bruce, T. (1991) *Time To Play*, London: Hodder and Stoughton.

Churchill, C. (1985) 'Vinegar Tom' in *Plays: One*, London: Methuen.

Dryden, G. and Vos, J. (1994) *The Learning Revolution*, Aylesbury, Buckinghamshire: Accelerated Learning Systems.

Erikson, E. H. (1965) *Childhood and Society*, Harmondsworth: Pelican.

Esslin, M. (1987) *The Field of Dreams*, London: Methuen.

Foster, J. 'Four o'clock Friday', in *Voices One*, Harmondsworth: Penguin Books.

Freud, S. (1959) (trans I. F. Grant-Duff) 'Creative Writers and Day-Dreaming', in J. Strachey (ed.) *The Standard Edition of the Complete Psychological Works of Sigmund Freud*, Volume IX, London: Institute of Psycho-Analysis and The Hogarth Press.

Galton, M. and Williamson, J. (1992) *Group Work in the Primary School*, London: Routledge.

Garvey, C. (1976) 'Some properties of social play', in J. S. Bruner, A. Jolly and K. Sylva (eds) *Play*, Harmondsworth: Penguin Books.

Goleman, D. (1995) *Emotional Intelligence*, New York: Bantam.

Grotowski, J. (1969) *Towards a Poor Theatre*, London: Methuen.

Heathcote, D. (1970) *Three Looms Waiting*, interview in the BBC Omnibus series.

Heathcote, D. (1984) *Collected Writings*, London: Hutchinson.

Hornbrook, D. (1989) *Education and Dramatic Art*, Oxford: Blackwell.

Hornbrook, D. (1991) *Education in Drama: Casting the Dramatic Curriculum*, London: Falmer Press.

Huizinga, J. (1970) *Homo Ludens*, London: Paladin.

Hutt, S. J., Tyler, S., Hutt, C. and Christopherson, H. (1989) *Play, Exploration and Learning*, London: Routledge.

Kitson, N. (1994) '"Please Miss Alexander, will you be the robber!" Fantasy play – the case for adult intervention', in J. Moyles (ed.) *The Excellence of Play*, Milton Keynes: Open University Press.

Kitson, N. and Spiby, I. (1989) *Drama Conventions: A Second DIY Guide*, BBC Education.

Kitson, N. and Spiby, I. (1995) *Primary Drama Handbook*, London: Watts Publishers.

Klugman, E. and Smilansky, S. (1990) *Children's Play: Perspectives and Policy Implications*, New York: Teacher's College Press.

Manning, K. and Sharp, A. (1977) *Structuring Play*, London: Ward Lock.

Miller, A. (1949 (1961)) *Death of a Salesman*, Harmondsworth: Penguin Books.

Morgan, N. and Saxton, J. (1987) *Teaching Drama. A Mind of Many Wonders...*, London: Hutchinson.

Neelands, J. (1984) *Making Sense of Drama*, London: Heinemann.

Neelands, J. (1990) *Structuring Drama Work*, Cambridge: Cambridge University Press.

Piaget, J. (1952) *The Origins of Intelligence in Children*, New York: International Universities Press.

Singer, D. and Singer, J. (1990) *The House of Make Believe*, Cambridge, Massachusetts: Harvard University Press.

Slade, P. (1958) *An Introduction to Child Drama*, London: University of London Press.

Smilansky, S. (1968) *The Effects of Sociodramatic Play on Disadvantaged Pre-school Children*, New York: John Wiley.

Smilansky, S. and Shefatya, L. (1990) *Facilitating Play: A Medium for Promoting Cognitive, Socio-emotional and Academic Development in Young Children*, Gaithersberg, Md. Psychological and Educational Press.

Stanislavsky, C. (trans. D. Magershack, 1950) *Stanislavsky on the Art of the Stage*, London: Faber.

Vygotsky, L. S. (1978) *Mind In Society*, Cambridge, Massachusetts: Harvard University Press.

Wagner, B. J. (1979) *Dorothy Heathcote: Drama as a Learning Medium*, London: Hutchinson.

Watkins, B. (1981) *Drama and Education*, London: Batsford.

Way, B. (1967) *Development through Drama*, Harlow: Longman.

Weininger, O. (1988) '"What if" and "as if": imagination and pretend play in early childhood', in K. Egan and D. Nadaner (eds) *Imagination and Education*, Milton Keynes: Open University Press.

Willis, E. E. and D'Arienzo, C. (1981) *Writing Scripts for Television, Radio and Film*, Orlando, Florida: Holt, Rinehart and Winston Inc.

Winnicott, D. T. (1971) *Playing and Reality*, London: Tavistock.

Index

Victorians drama: use of conscience alley 65–6; use of conventions 63–4
volunteer-in-role 87
Vygotsky, L.S. 38

Wagner, Betty-Jane: on Dorothy Heathcote 16, 104–5

Watkins, Brian: *Drama and Education* 71–2
Way, Brian 12, 16, 23; *Development through Drama* 103–4
'well-made play' 80–1
whole-group narration 87
words/gestures: as signs/signals 96
writing: as part of drama 29–30